FUTURE LEADER

FUTURE LEADER

Spirituality, Mentors, Context and Style for Leaders of the Future

Viv Thomas

PATERNOSTER
PRESS

First published in 1999 by Paternoster Press
Reprinted 1999, 2000, 2001, 2003

09 08 07 06 05 04 03   11 10 9 8 7 6 5

Paternoster Press is an imprint of Authentic Media,
PO Box 300, Carlisle, Cumbria, CA3 0QS, UK
and PO Box 1047, Waynesboro, GA 30830-2047, USA
www.paternoster-publishing.com

British Library Cataloguing-in-Publication Data
A catalogue record for this book is available from the British Library

ISBN 0-85364-949-9

Cover design by Mainstream, Lancaster
Typeset by WestKey Ltd., Falmouth, Cornwall
Printed and bound in Great Britain by
Cox & Wyman Ltd, Reading, Berkshire

*To my love and my wife Sheila,
and to three future leaders,
Alex, Megan and Tom.*

Acknowledgments

I cannot remember who it was but one writer said that all he did was retail other people's ideas. That is how I feel about this book. If there is any claim for uniqueness it is in the reality that this book is other people's ideas filtered through my own life. Consequently it contains the strengths, weakness, passions, blind spots, stories and abstractions that go through my own head. I gladly own all of them. I have many debts! I owe a huge debt to my friends and fellow leaders in Operation Mobilisation. I thought I would mention a few but the list is impossibly long. I need to say a huge thank you to Sirpa Manninen, she worked for me and knows this text better than I do having worked through it in detail. Without her endurance and intelligence this book would have waited in the wings for a long time. Jenny Taylor has done a great job in editing the text. Julia Taylor stepped in at a crucial time and handled all sorts of things for me. Finally, a debt which can never be repaid to Rob and Brenda, brother and sister, love and fire.

Contents

Part III: Mentors for the future

Part IV: Leaders for the future

Part V: The process of restoration

Foreword

Leadership! – what an audacious thought! How can anyone aspire to lead into the future? With the high speed of change brought about by rapid developments in technology and connectivity, the future looks blurred. Too much is happening too fast. Which future, which direction does the leader pursue? And who is being led? The boundary between leader and follower is hard to identify. Leaders may or may not have more information or expertise than those for whom they are responsible. And the expectations of multiple constituencies with varying levels of competence and commitment pulls or pushes the leader simultaneously in diverse directions. To whom is the leader accountable? The board? The shareholders? The staff? The clients/customers? The church? The professional or monitoring agency? The broader society? The government? To some extent the leader is accountable to them all, and that is part of the problem. How can one possibly succeed in leadership? Even the measures of 'success' in leadership are ambiguous. It is a prophetic service. The events and outcomes of tomorrow will determine the 'success' of leadership today. And that judgement will reflect the wisdom or perspective of that person at that time with a particular set of expectations. In the middle of this swirling cauldron of change and ambiguity stand the leaders, painfully aware of personal frailty and vulnerability, the words of the great leader of the Exodus echoing in their mind: 'Who am I?'

That is where Viv Thomas has it right! 'Who am I?' is the wrong question. The only appropriate question with which to begin the service of leadership is: 'Who is God?' Biblical leadership starts first and foremost with a person's relationship with God.

Leadership from a biblical perspective is much more about following than about leading. It starts first with the leader's dependence upon God. Only when the reign of God is truly acknowledged, only when 'leaders' recognize themselves as 'followers' of the one who is king, can we look for biblical leadership. Leadership begins in a relationship between a person and God.

Grounded in that relationship, biblical leadership finds expression in the character of the leader, what Viv Thomas calls 'inscape'. Finding oneself in the hand of God, seeing oneself in the spotlight of God's forgiving love, shapes that mixture of confidence and humility, love and justice that lives out the fruit of the spirit of God in every organizational relationship of service.

And that is precisely what leadership is: a relationship of service – a relationship between leaders and followers in which leaders invest themselves in the well-being, growth and contribution of those for whom they are responsible within the organization. Leadership is about relationships – a relationship with God that defines all of our relationships with those around us and shapes our vision for the future.

The future demands vision from its leaders. But not as much a vision of where we are going, as a vision of whose path we are following. Tomorrow may offer exciting alternatives and wondrous opportunities, but we may not see them until we stumble over them. Visionary leadership from a biblical perspective is about prayer – listening to God, about obedience – joining in what God is doing, and about integrity – following faithfully with humility and vulnerability.

Viv Thomas writes as an experienced leader trying to make sense of the service to which God has called him as he ponders the leaders of biblical history and reflects on those who have led him. He leads us to the only appropriate posture for kingdom leadership in the 21st century: not sitting in the office of chief executive, but kneeling in a community of prayer as an obedient follower of Jesus Christ. May this book give you the courage to let God lead through you.

Walter Wright – President of Regents College, Vancouver

Introduction

What is the point in reading another book on leadership? A good question, which needs to be answered clearly. My short answer is that you need all the help you can get when you become a leader, and this book will give you lots of it. My longer answer is that leaders are important people. If leaders don't lead well, then things go wrong for lots of other people. If leaders do their job adequately, then all sorts of wonderful, imaginative and successful things can happen. Most delight and pain in our communities and organizations can be traced back to some leader or other who either shaped us directly or indirectly. The leaders we have followed either consciously or sub-consciously have had huge influence over what we think, how we react, the friends we choose and the way we see the world. Leaders are very powerful people.

How will reading this book help you to lead better? I think reading this book will help you grasp some of the essence of leadership and assist you in answering key questions like: What is intended to drive and motivate leaders? What are God's priorities for leaders? What do I need to get into position if I am to lead well in the future? I am going to introduce you to some great leaders and indicate what sort of leaders we will need over the next ten years. Writing this has been a motivating, tough and exciting experience, a little like leadership itself. Let me tell you my story.

Leadership fell on me in the summer of 1973. I had turned twenty-one years old in March that year and, like many of the experiences of my life, the pain came a little early.

I had just finished two years at a denominational college intending to produce pastors and I was ready to go and lead a church somewhere in the United Kingdom. I was not ready for what did happen. I was asked if I would go to a working-class suburb of Manchester and plant a church on a housing estate. I could have said no, but that was not the culture of the denomination so off I went to do the job. What followed was a series of disasters, flukes, hilarities, excitements and wonders. It was like getting on a roller-coaster ride but without the opportunity to get off in a few minutes' time.

The 'church' I was to lead was intended to emerge from a tent campaign which had taken place in the centre of the town. I was not able to be at this two-week event, but it seemed to have gone well. Over a hundred people had indicated that they wanted to become Christians, and my first job was to visit them. I began this work with enthusiasm and enormous naïveté. I knew that not all of them had become Christians but I hoped that fifteen to twenty had. Not for the first time in my life I was over-optimistic. Many could not remember being in the tent, even though they had signed the card I had in my hand. Many were glad to see me go because the encounter was embarrassing; only one claimed to have become a Christian and she proved to be unusual and quite invasive in her own blue-rinse sort of way. She eventually settled for a mix of Jesus and Egyptian mysticism, which bewildered me.

I had John as a companion for a few weeks. He was rock-solid as always. We had to sleep in the church, as there was nowhere for me to stay. I fell through the canvas camp bed I was sleeping on, so from then on it was the floor. We did not have much money and ate a lot of corn flakes and lettuce. It was a sad day when John left and I knew I was on my own from then on.

Four people came to the first Sunday meeting. Two of them had a combined age of about 160, and one of them was brought in by her husband, who promptly left. She was suffering from serious multiple sclerosis. All those ladies loved Jesus with all their hearts. I can still remember the appalling way we sang 'I Surrender All', more like screeching tyres than worshipping Christians.

One family showed me a lot of love and kindness and eventually I went to live with them. This was the beginning of a wonderful and fruitful relationship. Other superb relationships developed, and slowly the church was built, mostly through weakness and intensive learning. My sense of inadequacy was huge, but God was clearly in the middle of the chaos of it all. Surprisingly, at least to me, leadership and inadequacy became a clear theme in my twenties and still remains today.

Christian leaders are generally a collection of inadequates and most of them, I think the best of them, agree that is so. This understanding of their predicament is the source of their strength, flexibility and power. Why is this so? The Christian gospel is full of paradox. The Christian leader is strong when weak, rich when poor, an adult when a child and in control when not in charge. This is a contradictory world which seems, at least at first glance, to be complete and utter nonsense, a little like the gospel itself.

Our popular western culture insists that to be first is to be best and only those who excel are able to become icons of our age. All who do not attain this stage of excellence and domination are considered inadequate.[1] It is here that the gospel kicks in and insists that inadequacy is the truth about us all. Even at our best we do not understand what is going on around us. The most excellent among us are so for a short time only while their skill or charisma lasts. Great Christian leaders grasp and embrace this, submitting themselves to its impact.

The founder of Tear Fund used to tell the story of a nurse who left England and went to work in Kampuchea. Within her first year she found herself on her knees with a bucket of water and a scrubbing brush, cleaning a huge aircraft hanger. It was to become a mortuary for the people slaughtered in the war. While she was scrubbing, a government official came alongside her and said, 'I would not do that for a thousand dollars.' She replied, 'Neither would I'! She had found something more fundamental than being perceived to be the best or as having the most. She was learning to live a submissive life, a life of giving to God, a life that was not negotiable.

The great Christian leaders are identified by the quality of their conversation with God. When this conversation develops, you learn two things: firstly, you are not much good at what you do; secondly, that's all right with God. He can cope with the mess of having you around. The effect of this acceptance of your inadequacy is to release you from the pressure to please the people you lead, because this is usually impossible, and to throw you towards God's grace, which is essential. Our adequacy comes from the grace brought to us through our walk with God, and not from the gifts or drive with which we may have been born. The paradox is this: Christian leaders may be inadequate, but understanding this places them in a position of adequacy. Stunningly, at least from a modern western understanding, it is the Christian Church which has been the most 'successful' organization in the whole of human history to date.[2]

If this is true, then what is happening in the inner world of leaders, their 'inscape,' is pivotal to how they lead.[3] Identity comes out of relationship, and quality leadership emerges from both. It is also important to understand how they see the world around them, their vision. The nature of their relationships is crucial in understanding how they lead. Linked closely with this is the way in which they seek to motivate the people around them and how they respond to their various tasks. This is the scope of this book, and it is everything I wish I had known in 1973. I think it is really unlikely that I would have understood this, but at least I would have had something to place alongside my walk and talk as a leader.

Part I

Spirituality for the Future

1

Jesus and Pilate: Matthew 27:11–31

> But Jesus made no reply, not even to a single charge - to the
> great amazement of the governor.
>
> Matthew 27:14

'Leadership,' as understood in modern western popular culture, is not reflected with any real definition in the New Testament; it is not a New Testament word. There are clearly
leaders who function as prophets, apostles, teachers, dea-
cons, elders, etc., but none who fit the present-day secular
model marked by a combination of individualism,
self-dependence, task orientation, supposed objectivity and
personal ambition. We have therefore a significant problem. How can we develop leaders who are going to be
rooted in biblical revelation unphased by the requirements
of popular western culture?

In Matthew 27:11–31 there is an encounter of two leaders, Pilate and Jesus. It is almost as if Pilate were to become
the final image as to why the cross is needed. This is the final
significant dialogue that Jesus engages in before he goes to
the cross, and the whole conversation is explaining why
redemption is essential.

The encounter is dominated by the subtext of leaders and
their vastly different worlds. The discussion reveals the very
different agendas of Pilate and Jesus. Pilate tries to make

some sort of psychological contact and fails.[1] He is sitting on the judge's seat, yet he is the one being judged.[2] Pilate wants Jesus to understand the difficulty he is in, unaware of the nature of the relationship and the problems that face him.[3] John, who gives a fuller account of what Jesus said, explains that Jesus is totally aware that this is a clash of kingdoms and the leaders of those kingdoms.[4] They both represent their worlds: they are the obvious consequences of the worlds in which they have been rooted, demonstrating what sort of leaders they are in the context of Pilate's theatrical political gamesmanship.[5]

What emerges is two models of leadership representing two different worlds and ways of thinking. What are their characteristics?

Pilate, the leader without an internal shape

A *victim of various pressures*

Pilate appears to be in this position of power but has no personal authority. He is amorphous: a man who could be moved into any shape. His life is a series of pieces that are put together by others, i.e., the chief priests, the elders,[6] the crowd,[7] his wife,[8] and probably the constituency in Rome, Caesar himself. It appears that Pilate shapes his personality out of the opinion of others. He is manipulated by the very people he intends to lead. This trend is well developed today with the emphasis on image and the power of the consumer. The great betrayal is that just giving people what they want is often reflecting back to them their own emptiness, thus ensuring the leader's life is also vacuous, just fragments gathered together for certain public displays.

The vulnerability of many Christian leaders in this area is clear. Our leaders are asked to serve a series of constituencies:

the family, God, personal financial supporters, the board, the denomination, the boss, and his or her own team. How many are really able to cope with this intensity? How many fail in their internal world and we remain ignorant of the process of deterioration? If we measure them by what they do rather than who they are, we will just intensify the shattering.

Rootless and disconnected

Pilate is isolated, a foreigner in a hostile land, without community and apparently friendless apart from the support of his wife.[9] Pilate has been severed from his roots, he is at sea and does not know which direction the wind is going to take him. He is confused about 'truth,' focusing on quick solutions which appear to be tactically aware but which are without wisdom,[10] and unrealistic about his ability to control this situation.

His deepest fantasy and greatest symptom of disconnection is a belief in self-forgiveness.[11] Such was his feeling of power that he believed he could do what only God and others could do; that by 'washing his hands' he could avoid the responsibility which was clearly his.[12] Pilate had become his own Lord, able to live at ease with injustice which follows from this assumption.

Jesus, the leader with the fully-formed internal life

Jesus is passion-filled intention

Pilate is a personality put together by the opinion of others, whereas Jesus is full of purpose and resolve. This resolve shows itself not in his manifest control of the encounter but in silence. Why was Jesus here in the first place? He is committed to the cross and has no need to control this encounter overtly because this was not his intention. This was the journey rather than the destination. What do we do with a silent Jesus? This is disturbing behaviour, a God who will not speak. Yet, this silence is not without message, his presence fills the silence and he waits for us to listen and to observe.

The silence of Jesus is focused love and indicates the nature of authentic biblical leadership. We take up positions of leadership within Christian organizations not because we have a number of abilities but because of this focused love, the intention of a compassion-filled heart.

Jesus is relationally rooted

Pilate is rootless and disconnected in stark contrast to Jesus. In the middle of this conflict Jesus is living with a clear sense of his Father.[13] It is in relationship with his Father that decisions have been taken to bring him to this moment. From this a new paradigm emerges: Pilate is the self-made man, Jesus is the relationally-made man.

The design, intent and execution of the gospel is at its very heart relational. It is so because it is the reflection of the heart of God. Christian leaders living without this reality will become mere managers of projects and organizational functionaries. I do not think it is an exaggeration to say that the future of the church depends on its leadership being relationally-rooted people. This will mean an ongoing conversation with their heavenly Father and a similar conversation with those whom they have been called to lead.

Jesus is substance rather than projected image

While Pilate is determined to get out of this situation as fast as possible, Jesus is digging into the inevitable suffering. It does not appear that Jesus is in control, he is the one who is given over to the Praetorian Guard and whipped to the bone. He is spat on and has a crown of thorns set on his head. Everything says he is out of control because he is the one who is suffering, yet we know that the opposite is true. Why all this endurance of suffering? This was just the pre-amble to what was to come because his focus was long-term. The greatest battle was yet to come, as he was yet to be nailed to the cross and become a curse.

In modern western culture the focus is on the image the leader projects. The reality behind an image is rarely exam-ined. Suffering is not part of this image, but success cer-tainly is. Christian leaders are under more pressure than ever before to develop and enhance their image and the im-age of their work. There is nothing wrong in this, as long as the image projected is an accurate reflection of the reality behind the face. In recent years we have put a huge effort into accomplishing goals and projecting a face, but it is now time to focus more sharply on the substance and shape of our internal lives and relationships. The Jesus and Pilate en-counter was the triumph of substance over image, and we should be known for a similar triumph.

In short, the Christian leader should be driven by com-passion not addiction, rooted in relational life, not task, and continually building a substantive life, not a projected image. If we fail in this, much of what we do in terms of goals, strategies, skills, mission and communication will eventually be blown away.

2

The 'Inscape' of a Leader:
John 13:1–17

Jesus knew the Father had put all things under his power, and that he had come from God and was returning to God.

John 13:3

The appearances mislead: prayer is never the first word; it is always the second word. God has the first word. Prayer is answering speech; it is not primarily 'address' but 'response'.

Eugene Peterson, *Working the Angles*

Vancouver, British Columbia, is second on my personal and eccentric list of great cities in the world. The view from Spanish Banks across to Grouse Mountain, with the city dwarfed by creation around it, is a unique landscape. If you watch it long enough and often enough, you will see that it is rarely the same. Differences in the season, the time of day, the weather, and your own mood contribute to a continual variety of scenes and feelings. It is wonderful.

The landscape has a sister, the 'inscape' of the observer. There is a certain shape to each landscape and to each inscape. The contours of our lives, the weather systems passing through us as moods, the age of our bodies, the friends we have or do not have, our own histories and intended futures all form our inscape. It is the condition of this inscape that establishes what sort of leaders we will be. Jesus had an inscape; he responded to the external world through the frame of his internal world. What was his inscape like?

John gives us a description of the internal world of Jesus.[1] Before Jesus goes to the cross and before he teaches the disciples crucial material regarding the role of the Holy Spirit, the future, and prayer, he gives them a model of how to serve each other by washing their feet. But we get an insight into Jesus' internal world even before he washes the disciples' feet: the text says, 'Jesus knew that the Father had put all things under his power, and that he had come from God and was returning to God.' John is describing Jesus' inscape as triangular. He has an assured relationship with his Father; he has a clear understanding of his own history and is able to grasp the shape of his future. All great leadership is based on this triangular internal world.

'Jesus knew the father . . .'

Quality leadership emerges from quality relationship. The relationship between Father, Son and Holy Spirit is set in profound mystery; yet it is central to our understanding of God. Jesus is aware of conversation between himself and the Father; he knows the Father and his approval. This picture of how God relates to himself is an indication of how leadership is intended to work.

Leaders have no choice but to be related to community, if they want to do their work well. Isolated and 'self-made' men and women are in the wrong place if they want to be trusted with the development of people. One of the marks of cultic behaviour is that their leaders often live in protected isolation. I remember as a young pastor being invited to a weekend with a well-known American evangelist who was holding a conference at a hotel in the English Midlands.

He was paying the bill, so I was very thankful for a free weekend. He was, and remains, a controversial character, so I was looking forward to asking him some questions affecting me and the little church I was leading. Even though we shared the same hotel and were in the same room for several hours over the weekend, I was never able to talk with him. The pattern was set from the first meeting. One of his assistants would lead us in a time of prayer and worship, the evangelist would come and preach, and while the assistant led us in a time of response the evangelist would leave. The evangelist's intention to influence young pastors through his teaching and preaching was undermined by his isolationist behaviour. I learnt one major thing from the weekend: do not behave like this man if you want to influence people for good. Leadership with a biblical shape is rooted in community. Whom we know is more vital than what we know.[2]

It is out of the relationship with his Father that the authority of Jesus is seen to emerge; Jesus knew that 'the Father had put all things under his power.' His authority is not rooted in gift or charisma but in relationship. Leaders tend to be powerful people exercising authority in all of its dimensions; they are often dangerous people. Gareth Morgan outlines fourteen sources of organizational power :1) formal authority, 2) control of scarce resources, 3) use of organizational rules and regulations, 4) control of the decision-making process, 5) control of knowledge and information, 6) control of boundaries, 7) ability to cope with uncertainty, 8) control of technology, 9) interpersonal alliances, networks and informal organizations, 10) control of counter organizations, 11) symbolism and the management of meaning, 12) gender and the management of gender relations, 13) structural factors that define the stage of action, 14) the power one already has.[3] For power and authority to be operated well, they have to be legitimately received and not grasped by an individual. Jesus received his from his Father; he did not reach out and take it by himself.

It is from our fathers and mothers that we receive our identity. They have a huge role in shaping what we are on the inside of our lives; it is with them, or sometimes without them, that our first community experiences are lived. Their effect on us is profound and mysterious. In the modern western world leaders are seeking identity from other sources. What you do, who you control and what you own are the three frames of identity for most leaders of organizations in the West. It has not always been so.

Jim Houston, the founder of Regent College in Vancouver was brought up in Scotland. He remembers that in the 1930s there was little emphasis on your profession as a means of identity. It was not what you did that defined you, rather it was your family. The fact that you were a lawyer or a doctor was incidental to who you were. This is not so in Britain today. Today, people are seeking to define themselves by skills, qualifications, profession, personal appearance, ownership of property, heroes that are followed, and money.

The identity of Jesus is related to the identity of his Father.[4] The initiative and execution of the whole salvation event was in conversation with his Father.[5] If we are to lead well, our identity has to be shaped by similar forces; otherwise we will become victims of our own gifting, a liability to others and ourselves. The adolescent leadership that can be seen today is due to few fathers and little community. Jesus knew the Father and great leaders know him as well.

'. . . he had come from God . . .'

At the second corner of triangular leadership is history. Jesus knew where he came from: '. . . he had come from God.'

Identity is not only relationally rooted but is also historically rooted. Relationships of quality do not just appear from somewhere, they have a history.

Each of us has a set of roots which is our personal history. We are able to reflect on friends and family, the joy, pain and burdens that emerge from our memories. I was brought up in Southport, England. My father met my mother in a pub. He came into the bar in his naval uniform and she was serving the beer. Six weeks later they decided to marry. They had two sons who were added to a daughter from a previous relationship my mother had had. Roy and Ruth's marriage was not a great one. They drank a lot of alcohol and fought much of the time. My mother was much smaller than my father, but she was mentally tougher and used to win the battles. She won through various forms of intimidation rather than through applying logic to her argument.

Jesus had a history. He was from a working family, had a father, mother, brothers and sisters, lived in Nazareth and grew from baby to man. However, in chapter 13, John ignores all of this and moves into another dimension regarding the history of Jesus, establishing that his roots and history relate to God as his Father. The experience of Nazareth is ignored on the basis that there is a much more influential frame that is to be understood.

What is being explained is fundamental to the task of leading. For the Christian leader there are two sets of roots, two histories which come together upon entry into the kingdom of God. We have our roots and histories from our genetic make-up, but we also have our roots and histories which emerge from the eternal purposes of God. Paul puts this idea of the eternal purposes of God most clearly, when he states, 'For he chose us in him before the creation of the world to be holy and blameless in his sight.'[6] Grace brings our dual histories together, and these two powerful forces form us into the people we have become.

Why do leaders want to lead? Many lead out of a sense of shame and guilt that drives them along to accomplish. Leadership position is seen as the one way in which a person's own vacant life can have meaning. Leadership is equated with significance. A whole industry has developed around this need for significance, and it has not been without scandals. North Americans and some Europeans have paid considerable sums of money to have their roots established, a coat of arms discovered and a potted history presented. Occasionally, when a company has not been able to find any, they have created a history to fill the void in the market. Leaders sometimes have a similar drive: they lead in order to demonstrate their own significance, even if their only audience is themselves.

Jesus did not need to accomplish anything to establish his status. With his history rooted into his relational life with his Father, his deeds were an outflow from that community, not responses to drives needing to be satisfied. This is so with good leadership. It is possible that the one who most wants to be in control is probably the one looking for significance through the use of various forms of power. A leader's significance will not come from accomplishments; it will come from a healthy relationship to history and from roots that emerge from God himself.

'. . . and was returning to God'

At the third corner of triangular leadership is the future. Jesus knew that he was 'returning to God.' He was aware of how his final destination, his future, like his authority and past, are related to his Father.

Leaders have to relate to the future. How they see the future is often the element that enables them to be distinct from those who follow.[7] Weak leaders do not think about the future that much and are often consumed by immediate realities. For many leaders fear is the dominant response to the future, and this shows itself in the continual return to the basic questions: Can I survive? Can my organization survive? These questions are often not asked openly; they are, rather, deep inner questions which surface in our reactions and behaviour.[8] They are part of our subterranean life, primal fears emerging from the deep, and causing confusion to ourselves, those close to us and to those we seek to lead.

Whenever we are not doing well, our focus is on the immediate questions. There is a loss of perspective, followed by a warped decision-making process, which then leads us into a sort of lostness both for us and those we lead. The only way in which this can be addressed is through an adequate perspective of the future.

Jesus is aware of his future and his response to it is similar to his awareness of his past. There is no mention of what was going to happen in his immediate future, even though this was going to be the pivotal period in the history of the world. No mention of the cross, the resurrection, the curse, or even the separation from the Father. All we know is that in the inner contours of his life Jesus is anticipating returning to his eternal Father.

The impact of this on how leaders live their lives is all-embracing. If leaders are aware that there really is no future to be feared, how they lead will be transformed. They will be able to serve without being dominated by consumer demand, take risks and not be dominated by the fear a loss of face, be wise without seeking to be smart and be relevant without having to be fashionable. In short, leaders will be able to live boldly because the defining issue is not popularity or performance but the knowledge of returning to the Father. Similar to the ancient leaders of Israel,[9] today's leaders are to be 'longing for a better country – a heavenly one'.

3

The Seeing of a Leader: Nehemiah 2

I set out during the night with a few men. I had not told
anyone what my God had put in my heart to do for Jerusalem.

Nehemiah 2:12

'The vision thing' is what pursued George Bush during his final year as the President of the United States. His problem was that he did not appear to have vision, and the effervescent Bill Clinton did. Bush lost the election possibly because of this lack of vision but definitely because, even if he had one, he was not able to communicate it to the voters of America. It was fascinating to see a similar encounter between John Major and Tony Blair in the British election of 1997. It seems that leaders are expected to have 'vision', and if they do not have it, it seems to be important that they behave as if they did.

It is possible to have a vision but for it to be the wrong one. A friend in London recently applied for a job which was almost his; he failed due to his inappropriate way of seeing. He was asked in the interview, 'Why do you want to do this job?' He told them that he wanted to see the lives of people improve and the world to be a better place because of his contribution. He failed to get the job. They wanted him to say that money, and lots of it, dominated his vision, the way he saw the world. The agent who had arranged the interview on my friend's behalf was in despair at his failure to answer the vision question without a clear financially driven answer and moved on to other clients.

I wept through a few sections of the film *Mr Holland's Opus*. The film is sentimental in the extreme but no less powerful for that. Richard Dreyfuss plays the hero who wants to become a composer. For a few years he decides to teach so that he can finance himself through the early years of marriage. His vision is the production of his *opus*. The fascinating thing in the story is not the piece of music he writes but how the vision is intersected, readjusted and confused. There is not much doubt at the end of the film that it is the children he has taught, the wife he has married, the colleagues he has worked with and the son he has ignored who become his real *opus*. The perspective is a biblical one; whatever Mr Holland's talents may or may not be, he is able to focus on God's focus, people.

The requirement to see does underpin great leadership. However, it is often not only what is seen that is pivotal but the way it is seen. The Christian leader can see the world as one huge project initiated by God, and see it as our job to push the project along. We engage in leading families, churches, mission agencies, and general tasks to ensure that the plan of God is fulfilled. Sometimes it is our very drivenness in fulfilling our tasks that stops us from seeing clearly. Often we cannot see wood because of trees: we are lost in the forest of activity without seeing the extent and nature of our environment.

We face certain blocks in sorting out the issue of vision, the way we think and the way we engage our context.

In the western world we think like Greeks rather than Hebrews. For the Hebrews there was no division between the spiritual and the material. Vision was not about contemplating good thoughts, cultivating lofty feelings and loving the universe. It was about how lives are lived in this material world, about how we react to the earth. For the Hebrews, doing the ironing and putting out the rubbish was as much in the realm of vision and spirituality as prayer and meditation. Our present-day neglect and contempt for the material world often warps our way of seeing. In dividing our world we divide ourselves and lose focus on what we are intended to perceive. This is a deceptive and dangerous route for Christian leaders to follow, because the more ethereal 'vision' becomes the more irrelevant it is to ordinary people. The Benedictines, who managed to think like Hebrews rather than Greeks, did not miss this lesson.

The story of Nehemiah is about the outworking of a vision in the rebuilding of the walls surrounding Jerusalem. The building task was seen as pivotal to national renewal. Nehemiah saw this very clearly. He did not live in a Greek and divided world; the building of the walls was integrated into the building of the nation. Nehemiah had worked his vision out in the middle of massive world movements happening around him. It is easy to read his story and think that the vision to rebuild the walls of Jerusalem was the only thing that was going on at the time. In reality it was only a minor story, a small context for significant things. It is only from the historical perspective that we can see the fundamental importance of the returning exiles; it was not clear at the time.

It is often the small and unexpected things which have greatest impact and the huge, and often expensive, strategic initiative which dies whimpering on the side. Vision often has to work away in this context. Deeds done unnoticed, feelings responded to alone and losses suffered repeatedly are the environment of vision. Nehemiah had it all, but what enabled his vision to become reality?

Emotional reality: living a full emotional life

Nehemiah took wine into the King, Artaxerxes, this being his job as cupbearer.[1] The occasion is an informal and domestic one, it is not royal theatre on display. In the middle of doing his job Nehemiah starts to get confused due to the King's comments on Nehemiah's sad-looking face. Nehemiah's emotional world and his task world were starting to collide with unpredictable consequences for all concerned, especially for himself.

Nehemiah's misery is related to the news from his brother Hanani that Jerusalem is broken down and the people who survived the exile are in great trouble and disgrace.[2] This news overwhelms him like some huge wave of sorrow and leads him to fasting and prayer. His inscape is in confusion as he tries to relate the news to his ongoing conversation with God.

This sort of confusion is the environment of vision. Vision from God does not come in neat packages. Confusion and emotion are acceptable parts of the human condition. They are essential parts of the leader's condition. When we try to block them out of our visionary process we render our vision powerless, or even worse, superficial. Stupidity is rarely confused; it is usually very self-assured. Wisdom is often in the middle of confusion, because it is in confusion that we grow and learn. This is why vision has to be delivered on a human scale and not broadcast for consumption by the masses.

This is also why many strategic plans stutter and fail; they are not worked out on a human scale. They are often like shiny glass buildings in the centre of our cities. Strategic plans are very impressive but are often immobile and intimidating. They can be slick, too slick to be embraced by real people. Shiny, well-polished, successful people embrace shiny vision that they hope will reflect themselves, but there is a problem. To embrace such vision we have to live with the denial of our deformity and project a perfect face; this is probably the greatest deformity of them all.

Frederick Buechner picks up this theme when he talks about prayer. He states, 'A great deal of public prayer seemed to me a matter of giving to God something that he neither needed nor, as far as I could imagine, much wanted. In private I prayed a good deal, but for the most part it was a very blurred, haphazard kind of business – much of it blubbering.'[3] In his inscape Nehemiah is blubbering. Externally he appears in control and focused, but his verbal presentations do not explain the confusion inside his life. Great leaders with great vision do a lot of Buechner-like blubbering.

It is the loss of control, the collision of emotion and task, which opens the door to the solution to his problem. Sadness and depression are strategically effective in this story. God takes the expressed emotional reality of Nehemiah and rips open the structures in Susa, which looked impossible to change.

Indiana Jones, for some unclear reason, had to find an ancient tribal artefact in the film *Raiders of the Lost Ark*. He goes into a cave, lifts the artefact from its position, and then all the tricks and traps laid by the tribe who considered the artefact precious are triggered. The adventurer escapes, not through strategic deliberation but through quick reaction, good luck and enterprise. He tumbles his way out of the cave avoiding poisonous arrows, leaping over deep chasms and avoiding a huge bolder rolling towards him all the time. Such is the life of Nehemiah in Susa. The power of what he saw enabled him to respond with sincerity and guile-free wisdom to the opportunities given to him by the initiative of the king. Nehemiah's loss of control was in the context of a life rooted in God, but lose control he did.

Nehemiah is in touch with his world through living a real life; his release was through reality in relationships and not through the implementation of a strategic programme. It is important that Christian leaders have vision, but it comes in ways that are difficult to control. Nehemiah connects with Artaxerxes through living a full emotional life, not through an overt training programme. Vision comes from deep within, often defies logic and is usually very confusing. Through this, Nehemiah is teaching us that power is occasionally demonstrated in losing control rather than keeping it. Rough edges are human things and they connect with the rough edges in others.

Quality vision: lived prayer

Nehemiah was serving wine to Artaxerxes in the month of Nisan, which was roughly the equivalent to April and the beginning of the Persian and Jewish year. He has been interacting with the news of Jerusalem's awful condition for four months before his vision is expressed in public. During those months he appears to be living a subterranean spiritual life; the news has been buried in him and it has been turned into prayer. Nehemiah takes the difficult news from Hanani, is appalled by it, weeps, mourns, fasts and prays, and seems to do it all alone. Nehemiah's rapid, internal, urgent and silent prayer to 'the God of heaven'[4] is based on a huge internal world of burden, prayer and developing vision.

To have a vision of substance, the pressure which forms itself into the vision comes out of your conversation with God. Vision has to come out of the inner streams of your life if it is to be sustained. The public saw in Nehemiah an individual with anxiety, but what they really observed was a fragment of a huge inner world. Nehemiah is iceberg-like: only a small percentage of the reality of his life is visible to the family of Artaxerxes. Nehemiah has been living a life of prayer and conversation for months. What was the nature of this conversation with God? How did the vision and conversation interact?

Nehemiah's vision and prayer came out of being in trouble

How can you pray all the time? By being in trouble all the time. Nehemiah's prayer is rooted in all of his stress and difficulties. Isaac Singer once said, 'I only pray when I am in trouble. But I am in trouble all the time and so I pray all the time.' Visions have the tendency to keep you in trouble: they drive you on to thoughts and actions which tend to clash with other people's agendas. The power of the vision provokes pressure between people, and trouble is often the result.

Visionaries are often selfish people, even though Christian vision requires interaction with the holy. Visionaries tend to boss people about telling others what they should do with their lives. Families and friends are called on to make sacrifices so that the vision may become a reality. Houses are mortgaged, travel is embraced and long hours of work are anticipated all in the cause of the vision. Whatever else happens, it often works out to be a great environment for prayer but it is also a context of trouble.

We often do not embrace the troubled reality in which we find ourselves. I believe most Christians tend to think that in any church 5 per cent or possibly 10 per cent of the people are in trouble at any one time. In reality, this is not the case. Our human condition puts us on the verge of disaster all the time: we continually walk a fine line between life and death, sickness and health, elation and absolute misery. The people who are in the deepest trouble are those who do not believe that this is so. If we grasp this, we are able to live lives of glorious dependency on God. We converse with him because we know we need him; it is often as raw as that. Trouble is the environment of the child.

Eugene Peterson outlines three levels of language: language one, the language of personal intimacy and relationship; language two, the language of information; language three, the language of motivation.[5] Language one is baby language, which is full of goo goos and ga gaas. It is the sort of language babies use and adults use for babies. As we age, we move onto acquiring information and motivating people to do what we want them to do. Language one is the language of the child, the language of dependency, the language of need, the language of being in trouble. There is nothing wrong with information or motivation, but they have to be rooted in dependency.

Leadership language is often language two and three. We want information and believe that with this we will be able to do the work of motivation. It often leads people to believe that leaders are successful people who have no need for dependency, no need to be a child. It is hoped that the leader will be the most successful person in the organization so that he or she can be followed. Nehemiah is not teaching us this. He is teaching us that prayer, trouble, dependency, vision and success are all linked together as tight as a monkey's grip.

Nehemiah's prayer is rooted in trouble but remarkably focused

Nehemiah moves from his trouble and confusion into dealing extremely rapidly with the opportunity that Artaxerxes gives him. When given the chance, Nehemiah quickly moves from prayer to crystal-clear strategy and tactics. He is very clear about what he wants from Artaxerxes. He wants letters to the governors of Trans-Euphrates and Asaph, the keeper of the King's forest.[6] Through these requests he is dealing with his two greatest challenges: safety and resources, two critical areas of leadership interest.

Nehemiah's emotion overflows to the explanation of his strategy with such a rapid speed that it almost seems that his sincerity is to be doubted. To be in Artaxerxes' shoes could have been difficult: you notice your servant's sad face, you show a little sympathy, and, before a few moments have passed, specific requests are being made about letters, safety, time and resources.

What has been happening to Nehemiah? Guy Claxton in his book *Hare Brain, Tortoise Mind: Why your intelligence increases when you think less* outlines the possible process.[7] Claxton's research has led him to believe that if you seek to think in clear, crisp, business-like ways, you will not be able to think well in uncertainty and ambiguity. In short, wisdom does not come in quick bites but through a process of gestation, which takes time. Solutions are not often solved through rational thought but through a much more mysterious process of the unconscious. Nehemiah's speed of thought in strategy and tactics is probably the outworking of Claxton's process. Nehemiah spends months thinking and praying regarding the situation in Jerusalem, and then everything rapidly and intuitively falls into place. In this way ambiguity and clarity fit closely together. His prayer life and strategy were closely linked but not in a conscious way. God was making the unseen connections beneath the surfaces of Nehemiah's life which broke through at the appropriate time.

Detailed observation: seeing the task

Nehemiah returns to Jerusalem and a process of detailed observation takes place. He goes around Jerusalem at night, alone, in silence and on horseback. We have a detailed and meticulous explanation of the route Nehemiah took as he moved from ruin to ruin and picked up the full force of his vision.[8]

Great visionary leaders allow the reality of the task to work them over. Temporary visionaries move on quickly to the next task. Nehemiah allows the task to sink into him. He does more than see Jerusalem: he begins to perceive it, to understand not just the task but its nature. Visionary leaders do not just see, they observe and perceive. It is the detailed observation and perception that produces wisdom in the decisions to be made. It is this detailed observation that orientates Nehemiah to the task ahead.

This process of observation is immersed in silence. Early in the story Nehemiah is in silence as he considers the state of Jerusalem and enters into a world of prayer. While moving around Jerusalem he is in silence again. This selection of dumbness is vital for Christian leaders because authentic vision is never your own. The vision is intended to emerge from God and be submitted to him. In the light of this, dumbness is often the appropriate response. The closing down of speech opens up the possibility of hearing, and a more profound vision is often the result.

4

The Friends of a Leader:
1 Chronicles 11 and 12

"We are yours, O David!
We are with you, O son of Jesse!
Success, success to you,
and success to those who help you,
for your God will help you."

1 Chronicles 12:18

How lovely the elder brother's
Life all laced in the other's,
Love-laced! – what once I well
Witnessed; so fortune fell.

Gerard Manley Hopkins, *Brothers*

Leaders are to be measured by their influence on people.
This is the only way in which it is possible to sort out the
Hitlers from the Teresas. Charisma, skill, education and
background are all neutral in assessing a leader's potential.
Even when the arena of leadership is in technical areas like
finance or computing, the measure of how well the job is
done will be the effect it has on people. Technically great
systems which reduce people to less than what they are intended to be usually cause strong feelings of alienation
amongst those for whom they were developed. An irony

and a tragedy sometimes takes place: a wonderful system is devised and executed by Christian leaders but the result is damage to the participants in it.

There is a widespread distrust of systems that do not recognise the people for whom they are created. Sting celebrates this in his song 'You still know nothing about me.'[1] The song attacks modern systems of people management where individuality is reduced through numbering and computerization. Even after all the systems have gathered all the information, he proclaims with considerable exultation, 'You still know nothing about me!' Systems which diminish people tend not to be trusted even though, for survival's sake, we often have to work within them.

I have a suspicion that when I stand before God he will not ask me what system I ran or what process I completed. I think the question will have more to do with who my friends were and how I related to them. The suspicion comes from an understanding of the nature of God. If God is the isolated one, on his own and without relationship, then obeying his orders is the appropriate response. If God is Trinitarian, three in one and one in three, then the pivotal issue is not primarily obedience but relationship. I need to obey, but my obedience is worked out through my relationships, my interaction with my friends and my enemies.

Great leaders are usually part of great communities. I write from the middle of a great community which is at the heart of my organization, Operation Mobilisation (O.M.). Organizations by their very nature are betrayers. They shift in response to circumstances, time and leadership. Organizations draw you in with one set of promises and then inevitably start to shift around, often causing fracture between the organization with its strategies, policies and procedures and the individual. The very best of organizations behave in this way.

This is why it is crucial that we think clearly about the organizations in which we work. The organization is not the community. The community is much more subtle than the organization. The organization will come to an end, but the community spirals out into time and eternity. Structures come and go, communities of friends remain.

The strength of a healthy organization is not found in its fine vision or in the energy it throws at its tasks. Strength is found in a network of complex friendships and relationships, which is organic rather than organizational. If the organic relationships work well, then it is possible for the organization to be healthy. If the opposite is true, then a cancer begins to eat away at the cell structure and organizational collapse is sure.

The Bible is full of great teams and great friends, people who were joined in organic friendship rather than organizational function. King David had such a team of friends.[2] They were part of organized Israel but the relationships went much deeper than national identity. It seems that the nature of the relationship David had with his people works its way out in three dimensions: a God-selected leader; dedication of people and an atmosphere of honour.

A God-selected leader

The relationship between the leader and the led is complexity multiplied by more dimensions of complexity. There is a changing emphasis in the nature of leadership between the Old and New Testaments of the Bible as the Scriptures cascade over hundreds of years. The gifted community in the New Testament supplements the anointed individual of the Old Testament. Even though we have varieties of models throughout the Bible, there is a clear understanding there that leadership is a gift given by God. God selects leaders usually through giving them the ability to lead.

In the story of David we have such a selection. From the middle of nowhere this character arrives on the scene and dominates all of what is happening around him. He is brilliant, inspirational, spiritual, manipulative and evil in the space of one short life. Yet he was central to the life of the nation and much, much more.

The nation recognised David as the anointed leader. He was physically anointed so that he could be king with legitimacy, and God gifted him so he could do the job well. Leaders need the affirmation of God in their area of influence, but they also need acceptance by the people they lead. David had both. What were the characteristics of this two-fold affirmation of David's leading?

David was adequately led

David was perceived to be a man who was not in submission to his own initiative and idea; he was a man who led Israel while God was leading him. The demonstration that God was leading David is crucial in his relationship with his people: it enabled them to tell the reality surrounding the symbolism of anointing. God was with David in battle, God was with David in the encounter with Goliath, and God had enabled David to overcome Saul. David's ability to follow was central to his relationship with Israel: through this the people could see that he was able to do the job of leading.

It is possible for people to be misty-eyed about leaders and anointing. Even when leaders do a bad job, it is startling how often people will follow, often with enormous dedication. The anointing of God is the ability to do the job; it is not some warm feeling of being chosen. The self-anointing of a leader is not possible, even though many have tried. The person with the desire to preach, but who is the cure for insomnia when they do, the prophet who is consistently wrong, the administrator who causes more confusion with each action and the leader who does not love people are often self-anointed for the task. Israel could see that David could do the job of leader, and they followed with that sort of understanding.

David was rooted in his people's lives

Israel saw David as theirs. In the identification of David as leader it was important for the people of Israel to see that they were of the same 'flesh and blood' as their new leader.[3] David is rooted into these people and they into him. They cannot get away from him and he cannot get away from them. They are going to lurch or glide through life together; they are bound.

This sort of relational bonding is vital if leaders are to lead well. Great leaders are rooted in the lives of the people they have chosen to lead. This does not mean that they have to have the same gene pool (as seems to be the case with David) but that they emerge from the same place. We all need to be understood by those who have influence over us; we need to sense that they grasp our reality even though they may miss the details of our lives. When we feel we are understood, we trust the articulation of our leaders. They are then able to speak on our behalf on many issues and they are able to speak directly into our lives with our permission.

My marriage works in a similar way. My wife is bound to me, she knows and loves me thoroughly. Her influence over me is huge, her opinion mighty. There are many others who have greater gifts of persuasion, academic qualifications and organizational influence, but none can lead me like she. She is rooted into me, and nothing or no one has greater influence. She is my fundamental friend. We are of the same flesh, bound together, emerging from the same place.

David shared identical experiences with his people

If your life were in danger, with whom would you want to fight back to back? For David's friends it was him, their anointed king. David's friends emerge from the experience of living and surviving together with him in the cave at Adullam[4]. David fought with Eleazar in Pas Dammim against the Philistines; in a field full of barley they took their stand together.[5] These shared experiences were one of the foundation stones of the powerful team which developed out of the adversity of those experiences.

Intimate friends do not just come from exchanging cognitive information. Lifelong close relationships are usually formed in shared experience. It is in experience together, not just in discussion, that we get the full and vivid picture of the person who will influence us. It is in the doing, and not the thinking, that those invisible bonds which cause positive mentoring to take place are formed. Love and intimacy are experiences, not principles or concepts. If the nature of idea exchange is marked by personal passion and engagement, it is possible to be shaped through ideas in a positive way. But good learning is at its essence relational, it is to do with experiences shared rather than ideas understood. Good books draw you into the world of the writer, they do not just tell you different kinds of stuff.

This is probably why the western traditional seminary/college does not work so well; in the seminary the emphasis is placed on cognitive development rather than living an adequate relational life. Spiritual decline amongst full-time Christian professionals is often the result of the warping of the soul. This imbalance is often characterised by a huge intellectual life joined to a tiny relational life. The brain has outgrown the body. The rigour of the thinking process is tested, but the life of the community, the relationships, is often perceived as a matter of good or bad luck. Relational poverty is the result. Great leaders engage with the people they serve: they laugh, weep, grow, repent and age with their community.

A dedicated people

Leaders cannot lead without people to lead. Great relationships and teams come out of good leading and quality following. David's people excelled at following him. The nature of how we follow reveals substantial information regarding our view of God. All of us are intended to be followers of one sort or another; the vast majority of us have to be able to cope with a boss in most of the arenas of our lives. The plurality of church elders in the New Testament presupposes that all will lead and all will follow. There is an art in this following, but it is being lost in the West today.

I spent some time training an English couple who were on their way to Turkey to work for a multi-national corporation. They were young, enthusiastic and financially driven. They had no knowledge or experience in crossing cultures, and I could see that they were having difficulty in coping with the whole idea. I tried to explain to them the concept of humility. I explained that if they were going to do well in Turkey they would need to submit themselves to the culture and allow it to teach them how to react. This idea was something new to this couple and all they could say was, 'We just don't think this way'. They had lost the art of humility and lost the ability to follow. My bet is that they had a bad time in Turkey.

David's friends did know how to follow and how to love. It seems clear that they loved David, and love is prepared to follow. How was it that they were so good at this?

They listened with their hearts, not just their heads

David expresses a desire for water; he does not command or manipulate, he merely breathes out a thought.[6] His friends were listening to him and their response to his expressed thought is instant. They risk their lives to get David a drink from the well near Bethlehem. They bring him the water, but it is now too precious for him to drink: it has become their blood to him, so he offers it to God as a sacrifice.

This story hits at the heart of deep friendship. Quality relationships are not based on duty or command but on a response of one heart to another. The reason why David's mighty men were so mighty was that they listened to his heart and not only to his commands.

Much has been written about how to build teams and how they work, but little seems to have been said regarding love and observation. David's men are watching him closely because they love him a lot. Their observation of him allows them to know his heart and not just his commands. It is from here that great teams grow. The modern emphasis on teams being built out of an amalgam of talents and abilities is shallow in comparison to this world of love and observation. Enormous power is generated out of such observant and loving relationships, a huge amount of work is accomplished, spirits are fed, and life is full of colour for all involved.

Why is there so much disunity in Christian organizations and churches? I think it is to do with the way we listen to each other. We listen superficially to ideas and words, responding with similar techniques to our colleagues. We tend to avoid attending to someone's heart motivation and so cannot fully understand their words. When we perceive the heart and its motivation we are able to relate to each other in a much more fundamental way.

George Verwer, the founder of Operation Mobilisation has been my boss and friend for over twenty years. I have worked with him on his team for twelve of those years. We are very different men at all sorts of levels, and our working style is so different as to be almost dangerous. At times we have infuriated each other; there have been misunderstanding and confrontation. Yet, working with him has been one of the most defining and stimulating periods of my life. How can such a paradox exist especially over such a long period of time? I think it is to do with the way we listen to each other. Ultimately, the relationship is not built on doing, accomplishment and a popular understanding of success but on an accurate awareness of each other's heart. Mere techniques of management cannot begin to be measured against this. Heart awareness is what enables good teams to work over a long period of time. This sort of team does not need an organization to keep it together; it is much wider than any system and deeper than any strategic plan.

They did what they did very well

Even though these men loved and followed David they were not fragile. The picture we get is that they were full of robust optimism. They were skilled warriors who knew their trade very well indeed: they were able to 'shoot arrows or sling stones right-handed or left-handed'[7] and some of the Gadites who defected to David were 'brave, ready for battle, and able to handle the shield and spear. Their faces were the faces of lions, and they were as swift as gazelles in the mountains.'[8] These were committed, rough and loyal followers.

Good teams go through development. Although the best teams are rooted at the level of the heart, the way they develop in what they do shapes what they accomplish. There was nothing mediocre about David's men, and they applied themselves fully to their skill and task. In short, they worked hard at being the best they could be for Israel and David. The shame for us, as we observe their lives, is not the lack of gifting we have but the lack of application to developing our skills.

Although it is crucial that Christian leaders avoid the worldview that winning is all, it is important that this does not become a theology for underachievement or laziness.

One of the great opportunities God has given us is the discovery and development of our potential. We have a responsibility to steward our gifts and see what they can become. The reality is that many of us vastly underachieve and settle for a lot less than the potential offered to us through our gifting. This was not so with David's team of skilled and developed people.

David's followers had courage

The men surrounding David were men of considerable courage. They follow the inevitabilities of their love and respect for David and appear to be unafraid of the consequences. Eleazar ended up with David, fighting for his life in a field full of barley. Benaiah found himself in a pit with a lion on a snowy day, and two men risked their lives to get their leader – of all things – a drink of water. They display huge amounts of courage with little regard for personal safety. These men are fiercely loyal to their leader.

It usually takes more courage to follow than to lead. Following tends to be more stressful than leading. When you lead, you are able to assess the consequences and make a choice or guess. This opportunity is not always given to followers. They do not have the same information as the leader and do not see things from the leader's span of understanding. Followers have to trust more than leaders because often the choice of the strategy or action is not theirs. Therefore your choice of leader, if the option to choose is open to you, is pivotal.

Choosing the right person to follow will open or close your life. If a leader does not lead from an adequate context, then it is likely that some sort of abuse will follow. David could have exploited their courage and eventually he did so with his cruel deception of Uriah.[9] What is significant about David's people in this context is that they exercise their choice. They are not forced or seduced into following but were willing participants in the action; the drama is as much theirs as David's.

An atmosphere of honour

There is a huge sense of dignity and honour expressed between David and his men. Their hierarchy seems to reflect an understanding of an individual's appropriate place rather than a mechanism with which to oppress those lower down. They have a clear understanding of how they value each other and the hierarchy expresses this value. Good teams are built with such a sense of dignity.

The language of a team is paramount. How does the team speak to itself? It is clear that David and his team had developed an adequate language of honour and appreciation. This does not mean that we all have to develop militaristic hierarchies so that we can give each other medals or titles, but it does mean that we have to find eloquence in demonstrating how we feel about each other. This will vary from culture to culture and organization to organization, but it is important.

The Americans are usually good at this sort of language. It is wonderful to preach in America. I spoke at a conference in Atlanta to about three hundred and fifty Americans who were on their way to Europe. I had five days with them speaking to them each day on relevant topics. It was great. They sat all over the place, loose-limbed but engaged, the atmosphere relaxed. Many of them told me how much they appreciated my conversation and teaching. I left the warmth of the Americans and flew to England and then up to Scotland to speak in a conservative denomination. On the flight I was telling myself, 'Adjust, you need to adjust, it will not be Atlanta in Scotland.' When I arrived in Scotland

I tried to make a joke to my host and the leader of the meeting. I said, 'I have a little jet lag. If I faint while I am preaching, you will find the notes on the pulpit, so just preach on.' This sort of joke had gone well in Atlanta, but in Scotland it was received with the utmost seriousness. Just before I got up to preach, the leader of the meeting welcomed me and announced that I 'had already made my excuses.' I preached and at the end, the only comment I received was, 'Considering you had jet lag you were very animated.' In the end the speech and the silence of the people in the church reflected a sense of coldness and distance, which I could feel, and it was depressing indeed. Now, it is possible that I did not speak well, it is possible that I misread the culture and the denomination, but, for whatever reason, we did not communicate. My own perception of that group of people was that they were living with dumbness. They could use their mother tongue well, but they did not know how to communicate love, honour and appreciation. But, then again, I may just have been jet-lagged.

Good leaders find an adequate language of communication. This may be highly verbal or it may be delicately subtle, but it will have to happen if a team is to be built. One church pastor in my home town is famous for the individual notes he writes to his congregation, another leader I know expresses his love through his consistent prayer for his team. In some ways it does not matter how something is said as long as the message is heard. Understanding how you do this is crucial for understanding your leadership style. Without a sense of honour, teams die.

5

The Flair of a Leader: Luke 10:1–23

"Go! I am sending you out like lambs among wolves."

Luke 10:3

Motivating people is a key task for a leader; the way in which you motivate exposes what sort of leader you are. Addictive leaders usually motivate addictively: the ghosts that drive them are usually the ghosts with which they drive. These ghosts often look spiritual and particularly dedicated. A deep-rooted sense of fear can often masquerade as the power of the Holy Spirit and a continual quoting of the Bible can often be a cover for avoiding the real sting of relationships. Before motivation is attempted, an understanding of personal 'inscape' is essential. It is only then that motivation will have the context needed for it to be done in a healthy way.

Jesus told the church what to do. He ordered people around, told them what to do with their lives and how they were to do it. From one aspect his motivational style looks like the classic 'command and control'. He says, 'Follow me,' and 'Go into all the world,' and 'The harvest is plentiful, but the workers are few. Ask the Lord of the harvest, therefore, to send out workers into his harvest field. Go! I am sending you out like lambs among wolves.'[1]

For many leaders the issue of getting people to do what you want them to do is their area of greatest frustration. We should be thankful that this is so. The seriously sick organizations are those where the leader has no problem with motivation; everyone does what the leader says without question.[2] The techniques of motivation reveal the extent of cultish behaviour. All the tyrants of the world have depended upon intimidation and bullying so that they could get their own way. Jesus was not sick, neither was he a bully; so how did he get people to do what he wanted them to do? – a task at which he was not always successful.

Jesus gave the disciples the context

Jesus did not always give clear instructions. He often left questions unanswered and was, on occasions, deliberately ambiguous. Yet, this was not the case at the initial launching of the seventy-two disciples whom he sent out ahead of him. He gives them explicit instructions regarding money, clothes, sleep, food, forms of speech and handling rejection.[3]

In doing this Jesus is setting up the frame in which he is calling them to work. He does not just give them the call to go, he also gives them the context in which they are to do the tasks he is requiring. It is clear that there were going to be a lot of unknown realities for the disciples, but it is also clear that Jesus is ahead of them understanding the nature of the ambiguity that they will have to face. Good leaders understand the context into which they call others to work. When they do not know that context, trust is broken and lack of motivation sets in.

In 1973 when I was in my first leadership role and planting a church I was aware that those over me had little understanding of the context in which I was called to work. I was sleeping in the church on the floor and I wrote to my denominational leader asking what I should do about it. His reply was, 'Please move out as soon as possible as the local authority will regard you as a health hazard.' My expectation of those responsible for me was from that time extremely low. In the loneliest time of my life I had now found out that I was a health hazard as well, and no solutions to my dilemma had been offered.

Jesus communicated the importance of the task

'No repainting the flag pole!' was a maxim of General H. Norman Schwarzkopf of Gulf-war fame. It means don't just get people to do something, get them to do something which matters, and they will be motivated. The disciples knew that what they were doing mattered immensely. Jesus lists the places which have or will have the judgement of God: Korazin, Bethsaida and Capernaum. He explains that if Tyre and Sidon had seen what they had seen they would have repented long ago sitting in sackcloth and ashes.[4]

Leaders who fail to explain the vital place of each member of their team in the overall strategy will have to learn to deal with demotivation. If someone does not have a vital part to play, should they even be on your team? Possibly they should move on to a better environment for them and for you. Some of the most trivial tasks are crucial in accomplishing an ambition or fulfilling a vision. It is normally the people appearing to be the least gifted who need to hear regularly how vital their job is.

Jesus identified himself with the team

Jesus tied how people perceived him to the behaviour of his followers. This is risky leadership. He states, 'He who listens to you listens to me; he who rejects you rejects me; but he who rejects me rejects him who sent me.'[5] This is an expression of fundamental loyalty to those who have decided that Jesus will be their leader. He is lifting up the people around him to the same level as himself. He does not distance himself from the results of the mission he is giving the disciples. He is explaining to them that he is happy that their failure will be seen as his. The position he takes is the outworking of his love and loyalty towards his followers. This means that the leaders are ready to share the glory and the pain.

The phone rang one sunny afternoon in 1986 and Julie, a colleague, was clearly upset with me. She said, 'Viv, this is the worst letter you have ever written.' She went on to explain how it devalued the service of good people and that she would have to do a lot of work to restore some relationships because of the mistakes I had made. I scrambled in my mind to work out what I had said in the letter, but I could not remember which letter. It then became clear to me that I had not written the letter to which she was reacting even though I had seen it. I agreed to sending out the letter because I wanted to back the instinct and gift of my administrator. The letter was sent out from someone in my department who was normally a brilliant administrator. Everything inside me wanted to say to Julie, 'I did not write it, someone else did', and pass the blame along the line to the person who wrote the letter. If I had done that it would have been extremely disloyal. I was the one who had said yes to the project; I was the one who put the administrator in charge of it; I was the one who took the glory if it went well, and I was the one who had to take the blame if it went wrong.

Jesus was saying to the disciples that he could be mauled as well. He had sent them out as 'lambs among wolves' and is explaining the nature of his own vulnerability.[6] This sort of loyalty and identification has deep and lasting results even if the projects and plans all go wrong. Even in the weakest team or organization potential can be realized at all sorts of levels if there is this integration between leaders and followers.

Jesus gave feedback and perspective

The enterprise of the seventy-two was a wonderful success and when they returned they were filled with joy. What seems to have impressed them most was that the 'demons' submitted to them.[7] They seem in a euphoric state of celebration. Jesus immediately gives them reflection on what they have done and the nature of their joy. He tells them that they have authority to overcome the power of the enemy, but that is not the point. Their rejoicing needs to focus around their relationship with God rather than the power which they operate. Jesus draws them back to the wider issues of their relationship with God and gives their success a context.

To motivate people you have to communicate sensible reflection on the tasks in which they have been engaged. This demonstrates that you have been watching, have perceived the realities, and have the competence and care to feed back the results of the observations. People develop deep loyalty to such leaders even if the leaders were weak in other areas. We all want to be noticed accurately; this is especially important in a world moving further and further towards isolation and independence. If there is a leader or team of leaders prepared to notice those around them accurately and express their observations in a comprehensible way, then that group is normally a motivated group.

The summer of 1997 was a remarkable summer for confession. I spoke in conferences in Hungary, Spain, Finland and Holland and in each of them I played the role which is played by Catholic priests all over the world. People came up to me and wanted to tell me the story of their lives, which

usually had some dark secret hidden in it. It was wonderful
to listen to the story of these people and explain that God
loved them anyway and that he could cope with their secrets
and failures. I was met with smiles where there were tears
and stature where there was collapse. I am convinced that a
huge part of the process for these people was being heard
accurately and that being heard communicated to them. I
enjoyed this immensely and, for the first time in my life,
thought that being a priest might have some fun attached to
it.

Jesus communicated personal passion

Jesus is deeply moved by the work of his Father in the lives
of the seventy-two. He is 'full of joy through the Holy
Spirit'.[8] The followers of Jesus are discovering that this
task is not only important for its own sake but that it matters personally to their leader. Jesus is not only vulnerable
to rejection if the disciples get rejected, he is also open to
great joy if things go well. Jesus is overjoyed because of the
audacity of his Father to reveal truth to 'little children' and
not the learned or wise. When this is seen in the lives of the
disciples, Jesus cannot contain his joy.

The way in which the seventy-two were successful affected the emotional life of their leader. He not only has
power and influence over them; they have the ability to
shape him. What they did and how it was done affected the
life of their leader.

This effect is an enormously powerful motivator. When it
becomes clear to a follower that what they do has an effect
on the life of their leader, they now have a new responsibility. If there is love and respect for the leader, new bonds are
formed between the leader and the led. What happens is
that those who are led begin to understand that they are not

powerless in the process. If what they do really matters to their leader, then they are the ones who have control, and the simple idea of leader and follower falls apart. This effect can be manipulated, i.e. the child pouting for a particular present, but when it is seen in the context of love and respect it is very powerful.

Jesus communicated privilege

I can still remember, with considerable embarrassment, telling one person who was working with me that just talking to me was worth £25 an hour. I was trying to point out the value of the working relationship and how mentoring was working between us. I failed to make the point and made an entirely different one, which was much more negative, especially as I work for a charity.

The point I was trying to make was an important one. The places we work at and the people we work with are places of privilege. We are working with individuals created in the image of God who reflect something of his glory to us. Working with weak, difficult, slow and sinful people is a privilege. Working with the beautiful, talented and clever is also a privilege. Each dimension has its benefits. The fact that we prefer to work with the beautiful rather than the ugly does not change the privilege of working with the ugly offered to us.

Jesus communicates the value of what his disciples were going through in their relationship with him. Jesus states, 'Blessed are the eyes that see what you see. For I tell you that many prophets and kings wanted to see what you see but did not see it, and to hear what you hear but did not hear it.'[9] He is saying to the disciples that what they are going through is very special and many others would have loved this experience, but it was not open to them.

Good leaders present this sense of the special to those they lead. This does not mean that they regard themselves as superior to others, but it does mean that they fully understand the realities of what is going on. The team or organization may not be the best, but it is a unique and never-to-be-repeated opportunity. When this sense of privilege and uniqueness is understood then a motivated group of people is usually the result.

In 1997 I was sitting in a conference in Holland next to two people, and it was a deeply moving experience. I had just told the one on my left of some of my fears, which included that at some point, due to the deprivations of childhood, my life would come crashing to the ground. My friend said, 'If it happens, give me a call.' I got the sense that my disasters of whatever nature were going to make no difference to the friendship; there was readiness for my failure. The one on my right had been through a difficult time in her relationship with her boss and we had spent some time talking about the issues. I had heard from someone else that my listening and reflecting with this person had been extremely helpful to her. There I was in the middle of this community of love and passion, two people to whom my life clearly mattered, and it was very motivating to be there.

6

The Task of a Leader: Daniel 1

Daniel then said to the guard whom the chief official had appointed over Daniel, Hananiah, Mishael and Azariah, "Please test your servants for ten days . . ."

Daniel 1:11–12

I bind unto myself today
the power of God to hold and lead,
his eye to watch, his might to stay,
his ear to harken to my need,
the wisdom of my God to teach,
his hand to guide,
his shield to ward,
the word of God to give me speech,
his heavenly host to be my guard.
A fourth-century Celtic 'breastplate prayer' attributed to St Patrick of Ireland

The book of Daniel is rich in material for understanding how leadership works. The book gives us a saga of culture clash, exile, political intrigue, evil, bravery, insanity, wisdom, dreams, visions, prayer, team, and the working out of God's purposes through it all. It is a mammoth book with many loose ends and ample confusion. The language of the book gets denser as the book progresses, leading us into an apocalyptic world.

The book of Daniel is primarily the story of how the Hebrews lived through all the pressures of change which were theirs in Babylon. It is specifically the story of Daniel and his friends, who have to lead the exiled community through the turmoil of the new culture to which they had to adapt. It is a story that helps us to understand how to manage change, or to put it more humbly, how to respond when change occurs.

Daniel is the central character of the book. He is the one who has to lead his people through the cataclysmic change of exile in Babylon. The dimensions of his task are huge and multi-faceted. It is pivotal to observe his life if we are going to see how he handled change.

Daniel is celebrated as one of the great leaders of Jewish history and yet he never was in organizational control; he was always someone's servant, responding to the agenda of others. If leading is all about being in control of everything, then Daniel was not a leader. He influenced Babylon through doing what he did very well. He was a top administrator with exceptional visionary powers, and it was the combination of these that seems to make Daniel so attractive to Babylonian culture. Daniel is constantly in some sort of turmoil and mess; there is no smooth career path for him to follow. He seems to survive through the power of God and the engagement of his wits. Daniel was part of a great team, one of the most celebrated in history; the stories of Meshach, Shadrach and Abednego are particularly powerful in the book. Daniel was an outstanding survivor, outlasting Nebuchadnezzar, Belshazzar and Darius, the men he was called on to serve. Daniel had a well-formed 'inscape'; various aspects of his prayer life are explained throughout the book both in the content of his prayer and in the style.

When we look through the book of Daniel we are observing a life loaded down with substance, solidity and great political skill. Yet, we are not looking at a smooth life because many things were confusing to him. His visions reflect the other side of his life where things are out of control and full of mystery. What is outstanding about his life is its authenticity.

I was walking through Bangkok in the fall of 1990 and noticed how well the Thai people were able to see the vulnerabilities of western values and exploit them. In the open markets there were shirts piled high on tables and next to them were thousands of designer labels. Gucci, Armani, Levi and Lacoste labels could be bought in their hundreds. The deal was very clear: you bought the shirt and then had the label you wanted sewn on. You could then fly back to wherever you came from looking like a cool guy. On some of the tables were Rolex watches. In the West Rolex watches cost thousands of pounds and on this table they were US$15! I asked the seller of the watches, 'Is this a genuine Rolex watch?' He replied with supreme unconcern, 'This is a genuine Bangkok Rolex watch!' In Daniel we have a life lived authentically. How did he lead the Hebrews through the change that they had to face?

Managing change: Daniel perceived the new environment

There are three environments which leaders need to observe and respond to if they are going to lead well. For Daniel that meant, firstly, the external environment of Babylon, secondly, his own local relationships with the team of Hebrews and, thirdly, his personal condition, his own heart and intention.

The external environment: the culture of Babylon

The Hebrews had been uprooted from their own soil and had to fit into the demands of Babylon. Central to their ability to do that task adequately was how well they got to know Babylon, its values, the way it worked and its anticipated future. In a similar way to Daniel, leaders today cannot manage change well if the realities of the world around them are not accurately perceived.

Knowing and perceiving the values of Babylon was crucial in eventually influencing this culture. Daniel and the Hebrews could see that it was a culture that had little understanding of the Hebrew God. As well as exiling people, the Babylonians took articles from their temple and put them into their own.[1] The Babylonians valued nobility, talent, image, intelligence, wit and the development of the best.[2] It seems clear that Daniel had an accurate perception of the culture in which he had to work.

I spent some time with a leading management consultant who works within a large university in the United Kingdom. She is a personal consultant to leaders of British businesses, and has a similar role with leading religious figures in the nation. In the course of our conversation I asked her, 'What do you see as the major difference between the Christian leaders you work with and the non-Christian?' She explained that the difference was in the Christian leaders' naïveté. It seemed to her that Christian leaders were always wishing that certain factors were there, but in reality they were not.

It will be impossible to manage change if we do not understand the nature of the world in which we live and the worldview of the people we seek to influence. We will spend our lives and resources in areas of insignificance if we get this wrong. During the eighteen months I was in Pakistan, I had a fascinating conversation with a Muslim acquaintance. I was trying to explain to him the theological differences between Islam and Christianity, and he was doing the same thing to me. After two hours of wonderful conversation he got exasperated when I said, 'What then is the difference between Islam and Christianity?' His answer demonstrated how deluded I had been throughout our long conversation. He said, 'The difference between Islam and Christianity is that our women dress properly and your women don't.' I wanted to scream! What about fatalism, the place of Mohammed, the nature of God, and universal love? It was clear to me that I had failed to read Iqbal properly. He had been more able than I to talk about theology, but I made the mistake of believing that – just because I knew his opinion on some important point of theology – I truly understood him. He was operating at a totally different level from me and I had read him poorly. Daniel and his friends appeared to avoid a similar mistake.

Daniel's relationships: the Hebrew team

Daniel's team was a remarkable group of individuals. What marks them out is their resolution and courage. They hold together going through assimilation into Babylon. Yet, they take huge risks on the Plain of Dura and eventually endure the fiery furnace. Daniel negotiates with Babylon and sets up agreed tests for them on the basis of the nature of this team. The consequences of failure are not clear, but presumably the price of not impressing Nebuchadnezzar could have been considerable.[3]

Few people are able to undertake a programme of change without a team of people who will help them through the process. It is important that the team itself is understood. Assumptions of what the team will deliver in a certain situation could cause the collapse of great plans and projects. A leader who is not attentive to the nature and gifting of the team they lead will have a rocky road in any programme of change. To overestimate the team's strength will probably mean that you will overstretch it with the prospect of collapse; to underestimate often causes boredom and disillusionment.

Daniel's personal condition: his own heart and intentions

The most neglected area in any programme of change is the nature and internal shape of the one attempting the change. We get an insight into Daniel's internal world as the saga unfolds. He has a huge and exciting life of prayer and dependence on God.[4] This seems to continue into old age because at the time of his encounter with the lions he was in his early eighties. Throughout the first six chapters of the book you get the sense of a sure-footed man who knows how to respond in all the various challenges thrown at him. Yet we know from the second half of the book that there was confusion, self-doubt and fear. A leader's vision is a source of success, a leader's fantasy is a source of continual folly, but the line between a vision and a fantasy is very fine. The key is having a realistic perception of self.

The price of not understanding these three environments can be high. The Cabinet of President John F. Kennedy was not immune from the cost of failing to understand the three environments in which they were operating. In 1961 Kennedy went through the 'Bay of Pigs' disaster. This was an attempt to invade Cuba which went badly wrong and cost the lives of many men. In studying this episode in American history one research body discovered that 'group think' had developed.[6] This was a type of group fantasy with particular characteristics: consensus at all cost, 'mind-guarding',[7] rationalizing, moralizing and discounting.[8] When all of these things came together disastrous decisions followed.

If the management of change is to be done well it will be because there is an understanding of the environments in which this takes place. Daniel and the Hebrews understood the values and nature of Babylon, which gave him the context for all the work that he was to do for it.

Managing change: giving perspective to people's experience

Daniel was going through the process of forming the Hebrew culture in the new Babylonian environment. There is no indication that he was doing this deliberately; it seems to have been intuitive rather than premeditated. The survival of the exiles depended on an alternative culture being formed, which would, of necessity, run counter to the culture Babylon and be subversive of Nebuchadnezzar's régime.

The phrase, 'But Daniel resolved . . .' (1:8) shows us what is going on. All of what he was as a man merges into this experience in Babylon and he starts to form a culture through his choices. Edgar Schein has written, 'Culture and leadership are two sides of the same coin, in that leaders first create the cultures when they create groups and organizations . . . the bottom line for leaders is that if they do not become conscious of the culture in which they are embedded, those cultures will manage them.'[9] Daniel became involved with the management of meaning. By his choices and decisions, he showed the way in which life was to be lived in Babylon. In doing this Daniel was filling the new cross-cultural experience with significance for the Hebrew community. This is clearly significant for the Hebrew team. They appear to gather around the initiatives of Daniel and go through the process of defining themselves in Babylon.

The leader's job is not just to give people a task, it is to explain to them or help them discover the reason why they are where they are. All of us are looking for meaning so that we can live our lives appropriately; it is the task of leaders to help us through that process. This is why Christian leaders have to be clear regarding the nature of what they are doing as well as in the doing itself.

People pick up the way in which leaders really want to shape their world and they often do it intuitively. A leader may be sending out one message in some sort of public relations exercise, but appropriate cultures are rarely formed through systems of promotion. Stephen Sondheim has written a song entitled, 'Children Will Listen', which was part of his Broadway musical *Into the Woods*.[10] The song is about how children listen and there is a wonderfully perceptive line, which goes, 'Careful the wishes you make, wishes are children . . .'. I think Sondheim is making the point that whatever you tell your children to do, they are able to see beyond the words to the wishes of the adult heart. He warns us that our wishes form our children, not just the advice we give them. We build our values into them and form their perceptions of the world through an intuative rather than verbal process.

Organizational cultures are built in a similar way, whatever the leader says. The real intention behind the words is what shapes the perceptions of people undergoing change. Daniel builds around him this wonderful team of Hebrews, not just because he did his job well but because he gave them a perspective, a frame through which they could live their lives. Crucially, he did this not with management technique but through the soundness of his heart. That his soul was centred accurately was the overriding factor, as it is with us today.

Managing change: making political and spiritual choices

In the new Babylonian experience Daniel has to make choices. These decisions were original to him: he was in a unique situation, never to be replicated. Daniel resolved not to defile himself with the royal food and wine offered by Babylon and yet he takes on the name Belteshazzar without any obvious struggle.[11] In taking on the name Belteshazzar, Daniel is immersing himself in the culture and taking the name of an alien God.[12] What is the reasoning behind the decisions he makes?

God had been explicit with regard to diet in the Levitical laws, and it is possible that Daniel's resolve not to eat the food emerges from there. There had been no similar instructions regarding what names people could be called in or out of exile, so it seems that Daniel has to innovate. With the Babylonian (and probably occult) roots of the name Belteshazzar, it would appear that compromise and accommodation was being made with this New World. It also seems clear that there was no struggle in the Hebrews receiving a pagan education, another issue about which there had been no clear instruction from God.

It is clear that Daniel was walking delicately. He was a mixture of resolve and compromise, purpose and negotiation. Daniel knew that God was working out his purposes in the initial stages of the Babylonian experience, but this did not stop him from making astute negotiated agreement with the officials who had power over him. He was both political and spiritual in his behaviour at the same time.

Spiritual leaders are popularly deemed to have lofty preoccupations far above the grimy reality of politics. It is as though you need to be distant from the world if you are going to be godly. Daniel seems to bring the image down to earth: he engaged in both political and spiritual reality and these had to be integrated if he was to lead well.

Daniel is not alone in this process. King David's reputation was primary built upon his encounter with Goliath, where he gloriously slays his enemy and does it for the honour of God's name.[13] We see him in a very different light later in his life when he runs from Saul and visits Achish, king of Gath. The reputation of a successful warrior was not what David wanted at this time, and so he feigned insanity: '... and while he was in their hands he acted like a madman, making marks on the doors of the gate and letting the saliva run down his beard.'[14] This is not a pretty sight. Where is the warrior king, the Goliath slayer? He is behaving politically, working a ruse, so that he can save his own skin.

Paul behaves in a similar fashion. In Acts 23 he finds himself in deep trouble before the Sanhedrin and God does not whisk him out of the problem by some act of mighty power. Paul develops rather a deliberate and divisive argument so that the attention will be taken off him. Paul causes the division before the Sanhedrin with a theological argument. 'Then Paul, knowing that some of them were Sadducees and the others were Pharisees, called out in the Sanhedrin, "My brothers, I am a Pharisee, the son of a Pharisee. I stand on trial because of my hope in the resurrection of the dead." When he said this, a dispute broke out between the Pharisees and the Sadducees, and the assembly was divided.'[15] This was raw politics in operation, and there is no judgement on his behaviour as being in any way inappropriate.

Bringing change into an organization always has its political dimensions. It was not possible for Daniel, David or Paul to be effective leaders without what appears to be the making of compromising choices, manipulation of the agenda and the withholding of information. We have to inhabit a similar world if we are going to manage change well. The pivotal issue will not be whether we behave politically but how we handle our political behaviour. Jesus gives us the context for working this through: 'Be as wise as serpents but as harmless as doves.'[16]

Managing change: understanding your authority

Stephen Covey explains the difference between what he calls 'primary and secondary' greatness.[17] Secondary greatness is to do with talent and skill: the artist who perceives the world in a certain way and can express their seeing with skill, the musician who can touch soul and spirit, the academic who pioneers new areas of research. Primary greatness is to do with character, the way in which we handle suffering, the way in which we love and how we serve.

The chapter ends with a remarkable picture of Daniel and the Hebrews. They are a combination of Covey's primary and secondary greatness. They receive the approval of Nebuchadnezzar and excel in all areas of secondary greatness. They are also spoken of as having 'wisdom,' which is a word associated with godliness in the Old Testament.[18] The idea is that these men were doing well in all the areas of their lives and had passed all the initiation tests of the Babylonian culture.

It is all the more remarkable when we consider the theatre where these men were called to work. All of their skill and wisdom had to be given in the service of a people who had forced them out of their homes, ripped apart their nation and were intent on using them in any way to enhance Babylon. Daniel had to live and work in a culture that was hostile to his own and only took notice of his God when it was in trouble. What is clear from the rest of the book is that Daniel and the Hebrews served this godless people with considerable poise and brilliance.

The task of a leader in managing change is often cast as a series of techniques which need to be demonstrated: have a clear vision, communicate well, minimize surprises, demonstrate your own commitment, offer positive reinforcement for competence etc. These things may well be adequate for certain types of change which are financially driven and short term. They are inadequate to effect real long-term change in an organization.

What is needed is what Daniel and the Hebrews offer us. This is not a vision of technique but of personal substance which is the foundation for their gifts. Such was the depth of their character that they were able to serve an organization which offered little back to them, and they did this with all their skill, wisdom and godliness. This would have been tough because the agenda of Babylon was not theirs and never could be. The eventual shock for Babylon was that Daniel was not working for Nebuchadnezzar; he had another boss entirely and this was why he could serve Babylon with all he had.

Part II

The Way we will Work the Future

7

Heading for Change

For many people change is hard work, and the present day pace of life is not making adaptation any easier. Although I enjoy and often embrace change, there is something in me which wants to run from all that is ahead and hide. Is there some island, some place of safety which will ensure security and solidity? When the stresses and realities of the world come pouring into our houses through the television and newspapers, do we not have the right to hide? The reality is that there is no place to hide from the future, it is on its way with all the threats and opportunities included. For leaders the implications are clear: we have to look to the future and see if we can prepare to respond adequately to what is ahead. The safest place will be heading into the storm, not running from it. We have to get ourselves in the right position, take a deep breath, think clearly and head out. Western society has gone through a period of transformation every few hundred years. As we shift from one millennium to the next it is clear that we are in the middle of such a transformation right now. Peter Drucker, writer, and leading organizational consultant, believes that these states of transformation are marked by the distance between the world of the grandparent and the grandchild.[1] Language is often an indicator of the pace of change and what is on the horizon. Language is changing rapidly; new words are quickly entering our vocabulary to explain new concepts. The speed with which new words and concepts emerge is telling us how fast our world is going. I was talking to some close friends of mine who are at retirement age and had just received a letter from their nephew who is in his mid-twenties and was on a trip to India. They did not understand many of the words he used, and felt in need of a translator even though English is the first language of all the parties.

This rapidly changing world is difficult for some to accept. When talking about women's ordination to the Anglican ministry, a huge issue in 1994, an English Anglican clergyman said, to considerable laughter, 'Why cannot the *status quo* be the way forward?' He was struggling with change and its implications. Some people hate, fight and find all sorts of ways of resisting change, but in the organizations of the future it will be the lovers of change who will survive. In the years ahead we will be living with faster systems and communications which may not lead to greater clarity, merely greater speed. The pace of life and the organizations we live in will be going a lot faster than they are now. We are going to be living in a world which we cannot control and which will constantly provoke and shift. We are going to need to address this fast-paced world with intelligence, humility, wit and authentic spirituality if we are going to flourish through it.

Charles Handy talks about the trends that are emerging now and will be well developed in the new millennium.[2] He says there will be a move away from labour-intensive manufacturing, which will go hand in hand with a move towards what he calls knowledge-based organizations. This trend is causing considerable turbulence in the western world today. The economic rewards will go to the controllers of information, the knowledge workers, and away from the people who sell their bodies through labour. This change represents a fundamental shift in global power.

Handy has three assumptions regarding change which he feels are deeply affecting our world.[3] He believes that life at the end of the millennium is what he calls 'discontinuous'. By this he means that there is no pattern to life as there used to be. There is no way of assessing what is ahead by looking back to the past. Things are changing so fast that it is unclear how valuable history will be in predicting the future. This is a little frightening because skills which are valuable in one generation will be valueless in the next. I may see myself as an excellent typist today but that perception of myself will be lost when all I will need to do is dictate to my computer and it will do everything I want it to do.

Handy is also sure that little changes can make the biggest impact on our lives, and some of the things we think are going to make a huge impact don't. He is telling us that we are therefore going to be in a world of continuous surprise as so many ideas emerge from the New World of technology. Ideas spreading around the world through new systems of communication will be much more significant in their implementation than was perceived at their invention, unleashing unforeseen change.

Handy believes that this discontinuous and rapid change requires discontinuous and 'upside-down' thinking, even if this appears absurd in the initial stages. Instead of learning 'ABC' we may well have to learn 'JU£AZ' or something similar. With the breakdown of the old rationalities of modernity we are going to have to embrace the chaos of the post-modern. If the organizations which we are part of do not think in radically different ways, we will be left behind wondering, 'What happened to the future and how did we miss it?' We can no longer think in nice straight lines; we have to learn to take huge leaps in the way we think and absorb the consequential confusion.

If leaders are going to face the future with a sense of confidence, it is important that we have a sense of what the future organization could look like. We can make some good guesses, but the very nature of the period through which we live could make these guesses look really stupid in three to four years' time. With as much humility as I can muster I want to suggest what the nature of organizations and communities might be in the years ahead. I am leaning heavily on the genius and wisdom of Peter Drucker, Charles Handy, James Naisbit, Tom Peters and Peter Senge; they have considered the future of organizations in far more depth than I have. Their books are easily worth the purchase price. Buy them and miss your dinner. What then could possibly be ahead for the organizations of the future?

8

The New Knowledge Worker

At this point Festus interrupted Paul's defence. "You are out of
your mind, Paul!" he shouted. "Your great learning is driving
you insane."

Acts 26:24

Knowledge today is the key commodity. The new 'knowledge worker' will be in control, dominating decisions and processes. The West is facing a new world of 'intellectuals' and 'managers,' the former concerned with words and ideas, the latter with people and work.[1] There is the development of a new sort of class, people who will manage intelligence and whose purpose is to be intelligent. As Charles Handy explains, a study by McKinsey's Amsterdam office as long ago as 1986 estimated that '70 per cent of all jobs in Europe in the year 2000 would require cerebral skills rather than manual skills'.[2] Peter Drucker explains: 'The industries that have moved into the centre of the economy in the last forty years have as their business the production and distribution of knowledge and information, rather than the production and distribution of things.'[3] The architectural landscape of the north of England is an illustration of this trend. The huge mills and factories are empty but the computer programmers are in high demand.

What is the nature of this 'knowledge'? Peter Drucker helps us by explaining that with regard to learning, the West has divided into two since the time of Plato. Socrates explained that the sole function of knowledge was self-knowledge . . . the intellectual, moral, and spiritual growth of the person or wisdom if you like. Protagoras on the other hand considered that the purpose was knowledge was the development of logic, grammar, and rhetoric. Perhaps today we'd call it 'know-how'. A similar division took place in the East between Confucian and Taoist/Zen philosophies. Knowledge for the Confucian meant 'knowing what to say and how to say it', while for the Taoist and Zen monk it was 'self knowledge, and the road to enlightenment'.[4] The knowledge of today's knowledge worker's has little to do with spirituality, self-understanding or morality. It has to do with information, skill and presentation and is therefore dangerously narrow.

The development of written texts to explain crafts without the need for a mentor wrought a profound change. The ability of the masses to read and write was transformational. It moved us out of the world of the oral and into the world of data. Through the process of technology and education the personal relationship between the trainee and the mentor was broken down. Knowledge was being separated from the interaction of humans and into pieces of information which could be written down. This trend was and is seductive. Leaders can begin to believe that the book is a substitute for relationship, the reading of biblical text can replace its application.

Peter Drucker says there is a trend away from a manufacturing base towards a knowledge-based economy and points out the significance of pension funds in the development of the future.[5] He feels that we are already in the era of 'pension fund capitalism' through the management of these funds.[6] Considerable power will be in the hands of people who control the vast amounts of money in these funds and the big players in this will be the knowledge workers.

In the world of the future the nation state will not collapse but it will be outflanked through knowledge-based 'supranational' enterprises and the development of technology.[7] We may see the right sort of government in our own country, but others from thousands of miles away could have a more profound effect on us than the leaders we have elected. This is already happening in the world of finance and international corporations. The power of Microsoft is there for all to see and experience.

Such has been the shift in our understanding of knowledge that 'educated people are not considered as educated at all. They are looked down on as dilettantes.'[8] The future will be marked by the development of 'knowledge' which will be interpreted as specific abilities to 'do'. The implications of this are huge. It means that if you can understand and work with technology you will have value to society, but whether you are wise will not matter that much. This is a long way from the Hebrew concept of wisdom, which had to do with the knowledge of God and community rather than the handling of information.

Interacting with this is Charles Handy's 'Triple I' concept.[9] This is where information, intelligence and ideas are the characteristics of good organizations. He anticipates that in the future, intelligence will not mean 'intellectual'. We will not have to be academic, just clever. Cleverness is like being good at sport, you have the skill or you have not, and it has little to do with your character or relationships. This cleverness, or knowledge, will be a new form of wealth, but it will not behave like property or capital, which were the old forms of riches, primarily because this new wealth cannot be inherited.[10] As Handy says, 'Intellegence is sticky'.

In the western world, leaders of organizations have been seduced into believing that it is the less significant people who need to listen to the wisdom of the significant. In other parts of the world this is not so. It is the senior executive who is intended to keep on listening and learning in Japan. 'The Japanese are more conscious than most that the other two skills of management, the human skills and the conceptual skills, are as important as the technical skills.'[11]

In the future it will be easy to believe that because you have talent and an ability to do something you will be wise and valuable. Feeling that you control the information as a leader will make you feel that you should be listened to. The biblical reality is that true knowledge comes from listening attentively to God, self and the community in which we are placed. In the future we may well be watching the Chinese and wondering how they lead so well.[12] Asian leaders are often more skilled observers and listeners than their western counterparts. Knowledge will have to mean more than just learning how to manage information to your own economic advantage. To lead well in the future there will have to be a tenacious rediscovery of the importance of wisdom, even though – and especially because – leaders will be swimming against the tide.

9

Emergence of the 'New' Team

Five friends I had, and two of them snakes.

Frederick Buechner, *Godric*

In the church at Antioch there were prophets and teachers;
Barnabas, Simeon called Niger, Lucius of Cyrene, Manaen
(who had been brought up with Herod the tetrarch) and Saul.

Acts 13:1

If we are to flourish in the future we will need some vehicle
for building this 'knowledge' into all the other facets of our
communities and experience. Knowledge workers, service
workers and everyone else will need the context of a community. For this we will need some form of organization
which will be flexible enough to absorb the information it
receives and continue to be transformed by it.

According to Charles Handy the 'Shamrock' style of organization will become the norm for all organizations.[1] This
is where a relatively small group of executives are supported
by an army of service workers who run the systems. The
third leaf is a flexible workforce, many of them being
part-time. Handy adds a fourth and that is the customer,
who is now required to do considerable work when pur-
chasing from many organizations, e.g. supermarkets, petrol
stations, furniture shops.

Then there is the federal model, where there is a coordinating centre and the practice of 'subsidiarity' throughout the working relationship. This terrible Euro-word 'subsidiarity' means in some ways the opposite of empowerment. In this concept it is people down the organizational hierarchy who hand power to central structures, enabling the accomplishment of things they prefer to be done at the centre.

Pursuing this idea Charles Handy quotes Homa Bahrami, who describes the new hi-tech organizations of Silicon Valley as 'multi-polar'. They are 'more akin to a federation or constellation of business units that are typically interdependent, relying on one another for critical expertise and know-how. They have a peer relationship with the centre. The centre's role is to orchestrate the broad strategic vision, develop the shared administrative and organizational infrastructure, and create the cultural glue which can create synergies.'[2] In other words, there are few walls between these units. It is difficult to know where one begins and another ends. The language and values of the holistic eco-warrior is having its effect on management models.

The future working community cannot be an organization of 'boss' and 'subordinate'. It must be organized as a team of 'associates',[3] but it will be important for someone to be the guardian of the culture and focus the team on the task. The nature of leadership is changing along with the types of organization. Peter Drucker emphasises this point when he states, 'Only when the appropriate type of team has been chosen and established will work on the productivity of knowledge workers and service workers become truly effective.'[4] This does not mean the end of leadership but it will mean the end of the old 'command and control' model. If you are in a war or in a life or death situation you will need command and control, but most of us live our lives outside those conditions.

The successful organization of the future will have to be an intelligent, though not necessarily intellectual, organization at every level; this will demand a new look at how teams are run. It will have other effects on our culture too because, as Handy says, 'Intelligent people tend to agree rather than to obey',[5] and we will have to work in what he calls a 'culture of consent'. This in turn will project a new type of leader who will be the 'post-heroic' leader.[6] He or she will need to lead for the release of others rather than to dominate or control. The new organization will need to be like a 'jazz combo' playing 'free flow' where the lead is transferred with anticipated ease in the production of the whole.[7] Service work will be contracted out and there will be less and less employment as it is understood today. This system of 'outsourcing' is already cutting deeply into government bureaucracies in Europe. Leaders are going to need flexibility in how they handle people and team structures.

Our new organizations and teams are going to need to be in continual education. In a knowledge- and service-based society the most effective teams will be those who know both how to learn continuously and teach continuously.[8] We will not be able to say that education ends with university; we will have a world of lifelong learning. The implications of this are difficult to follow but wonder, frustration and complexity will probably characterise our response.

10

Contradiction i: Creativity amid Chaos

It will become increasingly important to recruit people who
enjoy learning and relish change and to motivate employees to
be intelligent, flexible and adaptive.

Gareth Morgan, *Riding the Waves of Change*

Then a voice told him, "Get up, Peter. Kill and eat." "Surely
not, Lord!" Peter replied, "I have never eaten anything impure
or unclean." The voice spoke to him a second time, "Do not
call anything impure that God has made clean."

Acts 10:13–15

Demographic changes in Europe and many developed nations are going to affect the future. The reality is that 'in the richer countries, it is getting harder to die'.[1] The aging population in Europe will have to be supported by a decreasing work force and we will have to look to new models to help us. People who have been conditioned to life as employees will be expected to be entrepreneurs and many will not make the transition. Unemployment, as we have traditionally known it, is with us for a long time and we will have to develop new ways of explaining quite what it is, giving it a new meaning. It looks as if we will have a similar problem with the concept of retirement. It seems clear that we will need our theologians to help us develop an adequate theology of time.

When our concept of time and perception of what is significant are in flux we are edging towards the chaotic. The crunch point is the impact of these changes on people's worldview, whatever those changes may be. We are moving into uncharted waters, a time of considerable turbulence and confusion. Linear thinkers beware.

It is clear that the future is unclear. The only safe prediction is that it will be unsafe. Old ways of anticipating the future will themselves be obsolete. As Handy says, 'It is easy to explain things looking backwards, we think we can then predict them forwards . . . it doesn't work, as many economists know to their cost.'[2] The future will be so 'new' that the past will not be able to help us much. The potential for chaos and instability is such that it will be vital to focus not just on external knowledge skills but on internal resilience. We are on the edge of chaos, the 'time of turbulence and creativity, out of which a new order may jell'.[3] Mitchell Waldrop describes the edge of chaos as the 'one place where a complex system can be spontaneous, adaptive and alive'.[4] The way ahead is going to be both creative and chaotic, with the potential for new forms of fascism through to Christian revival with anything possible in between, and may be both together!

We are going to be living through considerable paradox, and Handy quotes Scott Fitzgerald's suggestion that 'a first-class mind is the ability to hold two opposing ideas in the head at the same time and still retain the ability to function',[5] a skill which will need to be developed. We will need to hold many opposing ideas in our mind and live with them being unreconciled. Living through chaos means living through contradiction. The Bible is full of paradox, complexities that have no immediate answers, personal dilemmas that remain unresolved, and even God giving commands which, had they been carried out, would each have collided with the other. God tells Abraham that through Issac he would bless the nations – then tells him to sacrifice Isaac. Abraham had to live through a time of contradiction where God was telling him two things and both of them could not be true. All he could do was live obediently and see how God sorted the contradiction out. All this is wonderful preparation for the future chaotic and creative world and an indication that the biblical world is startlingly relevant to us now.

We will have to be a culture ready for constant change, a culture able to handle continual chaos, what Joseph Schumpeter calls 'creative destruction'.[6] Unless this happens we will find that 'today's certainties will become tomorrow's absurdities'.[7] Our plans will embarrass us because the environment will have changed in which those plans were set. Handy explains that this 'discontinuity is not a catastrophe' but is the 'only way forward'[8] in a society which cannot see where it is going. This is not a bleak picture; people learn through crisis and the challenge of the unexpected. The times when continuity falls apart and there is no rulebook to fall back on are often times of motivation and excitement.[9] For many this will be the time when they find themselves alive, a time of discovery of identity and purpose. Many then go through a growth experience through the continual embrace of discontinuous change. The Bible is full of this: story after story of lives being shattered and blessed. If we can embrace the stories and see how God worked in them then we will be better equipped for the world ahead.

John Stopford and Charles Baden-Fuller feel that successful organizations in the future will 'be planned and yet flexible, be differentiated and integrated at the same time, be mass-marketers while catering for many niches; they must introduce new technology but allow their workers to be the masters of their own destiny . . . in short they have to find a way to reconcile what used to be opposites, instead of choosing between them'.[10] Drucker is very clear as to what sort of organization will cope. Each will have to have four abilities: the ability to create the new, the ability to exploit the developing new applications, the ability to build into its culture continual innovation, and a structure that is decentralised.[11]

Can Christian leaders adapt to this world of continual change? Are our structures so rigid that they will snap in the middle of this turbulence? Can we live and flourish on the edge of creativity and chaos? I think we can if we understand something of the dynamics of love and friendship in our communities. We will not be able to cope with the future if we just focus on systems, abstractions, power battles and money.

11

Contradiction ii:
Specialization amid Generalization

Charley,
Nothing's the way that it was.
I want it the way that it was.
God knows, things were easier then.

Trouble is Charley,
That's what everyone does:
Blames the way it is
On the way it was,
On the way it never ever was.

Stephen Sondheim, *Like It Was*

One of the dilemmas for leaders is working out what is to be regarded as solid and foundational in relation to what is mobile and temporary. It seems to me that perception of these things often relates to the personality and value system of the leader. Some leaders love solidity, and they find protection in emphasising what cannot be moved; others head for mobility and become unreliable due to their erratic changes in direction. In communities that work there has to be a combination of both the foundational and the mobile. We are going to need leadership teams made up of specialists who are very good in certain areas; the same people will have to be generalists, able to do many things in which they are not experts.

In the knowledge-based organization the assumption will be that your 'boss' will not know how to do your job, because individuals will have their own specialities. The boss will not have been doing the subordinate's job just a few years before, as is the case in many organizations today.[1] The effect of this is that everyone will have to take responsibility for organizational culture, everyone will be seen to be a leader as well as a manager. This will demand a huge shift in thinking because the question will not be 'What am I entitled to?' but 'What am I responsible for?'[2] This will be a radical shift for many people when engaging in work. No longer will the organization be perceived as parent.

Charles Handy suggests that rather than having jobs in the future we will hold 'portfolios'. He sees the main categories as paid work, homework, gift work, and study work.[3] He also predicts the return of the Irish village culture of his youth, where home and business are closely intertwined.[4] He feels this life will not be lonely because there will be organizational clubs, where you will be able to meet people who work within your sphere. Service workers will have less control than knowledge workers, especially when it comes to choosing work locations.

It seems that everyone is going to be some sort of consultant to everyone else. Many of us will be seeking to sell our skills in new ways and we will have to be entrepreneurs. Life will become increasingly difficult for people who cannot promote themselves or their skill. Yet, it will be important not to overspecialize because of the rapid change ahead. The specialist of today can become the joke and the 'has been' of tomorrow.

There is going to be an increasing need for people who will be able to bring teams together and turn them into significant united forces to engage in the task. One of the most significant leadership skills of the future will be the ability to integrate people and tasks well. These leaders may not be the most exciting people, they may be a little dull and lacking in charisma but they are needed. To be able to access these 'people gifts' we are going to have to look more closely at our criteria of what makes a leader. In the future the specialist will need the generalist, and the only way to work at that will be through continual interaction with the larger context of God, the world and the community. Both will need to be able to see the big picture.

12

Contradiction iii: Tribal amid Global

"I don't care if we win; just so long as we beat the Australians and the French."
Paraphrase from a member of the British snow-boarding team at the world championships in Whistler, Canada.

". . . all the peoples of the earth will be blessed through you."
God to Abram in Genesis 12:3

Some are predicting that there will be a continual rise of regionalism and a return to tribalism. It seems to me that to a large degree tribalism has never left us. It is not difficult to see this if you travel for long around the city of Los Angeles. The taxi driver who can hardly speak any English, but who is able to make an adequate living within his community, is a common phenomenon. In the cities of western Europe this trend is incredibly strong. In the post-nuclear age bigness is no longer an advantage.[1] Small countries can have economic integration without political subservience of one group to another. And people need their roots. The more global the organization, the more powerful will be the drive for the people within to search for their tribal roots. Our contradiction is that the forces around us are throwing us towards each other and away from each other at the same time.

In the church there is a model for thinking through these issues. We have the two huge concepts of the local church and the worldwide body of Christ. We of all communities can be leading the way in the conversation between local and global, tribal and regional. God has given us this wonderful frame in which to live our lives and there is a possibility for explaining to the rest of the world how tribal, regional and global can fit together in one community.

Freddie Heineken has suggested that Europe should be divided into '75 countries with a manageable population of 5–10 million – a very manageable size for governance – each with its reference to an ethnic and linguistic background'.[2] I have lived in London for more than seventeen years and there is a conversation going on about whether London should become its own city state and sever some links with the rest of the U.K.

Over the last decade this 'tribal-regional-global' process has been going on especially in the countries outside of the economic mainstream. John Naisbit has noticed that 'The world's trends point overwhelmingly toward *political* independence and self-rule on one hand and the formation of *economic* alliances on the other.'[3] All this is happening while many of Europe's leaders are seeking to build a federal state that will bring organizational control to the centre. It seems that two devastating wars in this century have produced a powerful force which seeks to blend all aspects of life, so that an enemy within Europe can never be identified again.

We now have the development of 'electronic tribes' with email and the World Wide Web as the tribal communication systems.[4] This enables people within one identified group to connect with similar people all over the world. The dominance of English, which is mainly people's second language, is being counter-balanced by an emphasis on mother tongues, which are 'becoming more important and passionately held'.[5] Among Naisbit's examples of successful future businesses, he quotes Percy Barnevik of Asea Brown Boveri, who says, 'We are not a global business, we are a collection of local businesses with intense global coordination.'[6] What will be the role of patriotism and the nation state in such a world? Is this an opportunity for Christian leaders to fill the void and build community around something other than nation or tribe?

Information and media will play a huge role in this paradox of global and tribal culture. Vast numbers of Europe's young are listening to the same MTV as well as learning English.

On the edges of Europe today there are major conflicts which could radically change all plans for economic and political stability. Which one is going to dominate, the tribe or some sort of worldwide community? The probability is that we will have to live with both and know how to move from the global to the tribal and back again. Could there be some new model, which would enable all this to be linked together effectively?

13

Contradiction iv:
Alienation amid Communication

Lord, Thou Thyself are Love and only Thou;
Yet I who am not love would fain love Thee;
But thou alone being Love canst furnish me
With that same love my heart is craving now.
    Christiana Rossetti, *A Double Sonnet of Sonnets*

In the world of the future, drawing all your personal worth and value from what you do will be even more precarious than it is today. Today is the day of the swift-footed consultant, and in the future most of us will need to have that role in one form or another. This is going to be tough because people are used to organizations and employers behaving like parents, giving them money, pensions, health care and protection in exchange for work. This will not be the world of the future, as it has not been the world of the past for many nations. Many questions regarding identity flow out of this context.

One of the great issues will be what sort of workplace communities there will be in a world described by the writer Peter Vaill as 'permanent white water'.[1] In the future we may not ever go to work as people do today, we may just sit at our computers and talk to people all over the world. Even in the 1970s it was seen that technology had the potential to disrupt 'anchors of personal identity'.[2] That is what is happening today and will be happening tomorrow. It is easy to interact with all our tools of technology and fail to relate to community through which we have psychological/spiritual wholeness. More knowledge and information will not deal with our inner anxieties and it is likely to increase them. It is possible that we will have hundreds of friends out on the World Wide Web and no one to have a cup of coffee with and share the events of our day. This shift, coupled with the trend in the West of many people living alone, will produce new and uncharted challenges to our social structures and sense of self.

With the ease of information exchange and global access, few things are now secret. How many of us are aware of the number of cameras we are observed by every day? What information is spread around the globe about us through computers and satellites? It seems we will know more about other people than we have ever known and have the potential to trust them less. We will be isolated and exposed by our technology. Unless we have considerable inner resources, our technology has the potential to strip us bare.

What sort of quality of life will be available if the 'ultimate in deconstruction is the solo performer'?[3] The picture that John Naisbit holds for the future is that of the computer shift from 'mainframe to PCs, with the PCs networked together'.[4] The trend is for 'the larger system' to provide 'service to the smallest player', with individualism, tribalism and globalism all mixed up and massive anxiety as the result.[5] In the light of this, Tom Peters, a well-known management guru, says, 'Read more novels and fewer business books . . . relationships is really all there is.'[6]

Technology and communication techniques are pushing us along in directions that are not focused on our emotional or spiritual health. There is a passion for measuring everything and this trend seems to be developing with considerable intensity. This is a continuation of what has become known as the Macnamara Fallacy, which says: 'The first step is to measure whatever can be easily measured. This is OK as far as it goes. The second step is to disregard that which can't be measured or give it an arbitrary quantitative value. This is artificial and misleading. The third step is to presume that what can't be measured easily really isn't important. This is blindness. The fourth step is to say that what can't be easily measured really doesn't exist. This is suicide.'[7] A lot of work communities will be collapsing and reforming all around us, our tasks will often be short-lived and remain unfinished, and the isolation and alienation will be ours. The most fundamental mistake that we can make in this context is to focus only on the tangible. If we build only around things we can measure we will live radically reduced lives. The human reality is that the most precious relationships we have are almost impossible to measure or even set goals for, unless they are very vague. In my relationship with those I really love, I have no intended outcomes although I do have aspirations. Most of the time I just love and we see where it goes.

14

Technology and the Way We Work

She seduced me; for she found me living outside myself.

St Augustine, *Confessions*

One of the major motors behind the chaos and contradictions of the future is technology. The tools of technology are shrinking in size, expanding in global effect and for people like me, powerfully seductive. Through a tiny laptop on my knee I can write these thoughts and with this same small box talk to the world 'on line' through the Internet. People have been empowered, rather than reduced, through the new technology. The problem is that it is only the world's rich who can afford to be empowered in the technological arena. In a very real sense technology is dividing us as well as uniting us.

Drucker explains that information, like money, owes nothing to anyone. It has no debt to pay to any father or mother, it has no roots in anything beside itself.[1] It is almost impossible to estimate the effect of this information and technological explosion in the decades ahead. There is one thing which is clear right now: instantaneous global communications are accelerating the pace of change and producing ever more frantic communities who know lots of things but struggle in forming adequate relationships.[2]

This technological impact can be seen worldwide in the sameness of the buildings around the world. There is very little difference between the new buildings in Tokyo, Calcutta, Dubai and New York. It seems that the assumptions in one culture are reflected in another, or could it be the dominance of the financial institutions which enables these buildings to be built?

I spent a day of meditation and prayer around the city of Vancouver and was shocked to see what had been built in that city. In my journal of 27 June 1995 I wrote, 'There is no acknowledgement of God on this skyline which seems embarrassingly out of balance with the majesty of creation around it. The mountains surround the city, the sea almost encircles the mountains. The very buildings themselves are constructed with materials which come from the stuff created by God. Yet it looks like a city built for itself. There is no circle of life, no taking from God's creation, re-forming it and giving it back to him in worship and praise. The tops of the towers are spiritual dead-ends. These buildings built solely for human pre-occupation, suck up resources and offer back no life. Here is a city built for itself; it is its own goal. Yet, the work of God is all around and remains unnoticed.' Vancouver is like so many of our great cities: it has a sense of self-indulgence and sameness about it. I believe that this is where much technology will lead us, unless God is at the centre of our scientific advance.

This worldwide technological culture seems to be dumbing-down the rich complexity of our planet. In one sense the world with the least diversity and richness is the world of the international executive. Pity the poor executives who have to interact with this sameness wherever they are on the planet. Many of the hotel and airline experiences are similar to eating at McDonald's but with the added factors of expense and attempts at sophistication. Many executives may be wealthy but they often look bored, reduced by the blandness of a busy life in the context of sameness.

Technology is transforming the way in which we learn. It is now possible to remain at home and get university degrees from another continent. The organizations that understand the possibilities of this cyber-education will have a distinct advantage. As Drucker states, 'The West moved into leadership throughout the world between 1500 and 1650 in large measure because it was reorganized around the new technology of the printed book.'[3] He goes on to explain that these changes were resisted by the Islamic world and China, which were the dominant world forces before 1550. Acceptance of the new technology is important but not as important as the purposes to which it will be put. Underpinning it all is the ability to learn how to learn and that learning will have to be lifelong.

Drucker places considerable emphasis on education as the basis for effective participation in the knowledge-based society; indeed, for him, it seems to overshadow almost every other factor. The cry of the Labour party in the British election of 1997 was, 'education, education, education!' In the world of the future, Drucker feels, the educated person will become the symbol of humanity at its best and have the ability to understand the various knowledges and their important areas, challenges and problems. He goes on to say: 'Tomorrow's educated person will have to be prepared for life in a global world. It will be a "westernised" world, but also an increasingly tribalised world. He or she must become a "citizen of the world" – in vision, horizon, information. But he or she will also have to draw nourishment from their local roots and, in turn, enrich and nourish their own local culture.'[4] This is a startling vision and right here is one of the great challenges that the future holds. How many people will be able to embrace this vision in the world where relatively few have ever made a phone call?

All of this raises crucial questions for people who want to lead other people. What sort of leaders will the new organizations and communities of the future need?

Part III

Mentors for the Future

Introduction

I do a lot of preaching and teaching. I travel all over the
world doing this and it is a wonderful joy and privilege to do
what I do. Evangelicals like good preachers. If you can
preach you often get room to fail in other areas and have a
fast track to influence. Yet, there is a dangerous assumption
that if you can preach you can lead. I have known really
good preachers who were very bad leaders; good preaching
and good leading do not always go together. I have no
doubt that we need, desperately need, good preachers who
are able to understand and explain scripture in a way which
is engaging and relevant. Our problem is that we expect so
much from preaching. We tend to believe that if people hear
the Word of God preached and their hearts are right then
this will be transformational but I wonder whether this is
really so? Even if it is, is it enough?

When I was leading a church it was deeply frustrating to
have so little effect on the people I was called to influence
and help. The thirty minutes they spent listening to me
preach was quickly forgotten. The thoughts triggered in the
message did not even seem to reach the car park. It seemed
that the greatest influence over most of my congregation
was held by their family and friends, not their pastor. Their
spiritual formation took place primarily in interaction with
those close to them: people who helped, understood and

listened over a long period of time or who entered their lives at crucial and vulnerable moments.

As it is with congregations so it is with leaders. The conditions needed to grow Christians are the conditions needed to grows leaders of Christians. Leaders are in desperate need of friends and mentors, people who will direct us towards God and show us the way. One good and able mentor is worth a hundred consultants, a thousand motivational or 'how to' seminars and only God knows how many sermons. Soul drought, which is the experience of many leaders, is often related to a lack of mentoring.

In this part, I want to introduce you to four of my friends and mentors. One of them is an academic, another is a missionary pioneer, another is a woman with two children and the other is a dead preacher. Watching and engaging with their lives has taught me so much. The dead one is an exception! He helped and inspired me through my reading and thinking about him. In this way the characters of scripture and church history are available to mentor us. Our leaders of the future will need to develop their skills with all the diligence and discipline they can muster, but their greater need will be people who can be with them in the process. Who are your mentors?

15

An Observation on Spiritual Direction:
Dr James Houston

Jim Houston is the founder of Regent College, Vancouver, British Columbia. He is still lecturing and teaching in his mid-seventies. He is one of my mentors especially when it comes to modelling the way we should live in the future. Jim Houston is one of a great community at Regent College and it is important to look at his life not just in isolation. Many other people were influencing me at the same time who do not get a mention in this book. I could just as easily write a chapter about Eugene Peterson.

Jim Houston's influence over me was brief and yet profound. God worked out our encounter in a special way, at least for me. I was on a one-year sabbatical in Vancouver having led a very fulfilling life in Operation Mobilisation with a mix of mentoring, teaching, preaching, shaping and travelling around the world. My motivation was high and I did not feel that I needed a sabbatical. It was only after two months on sabbatical that I realised what was happening to me. I had in both Jim Houston and Eugene Peterson some special people, precious gifts from God.

My father died when I was seven and along with my brother I became a survivor of domestic catastrophe. We both learned how to cope and manage situations well. Our mother's alcoholism thrust us back on our own resources such as they were. In my first pastorate I was alone in planting a church, which was accompanied by more survival techniques. In Operation Mobilisation I found many wonderful peers, brothers and sisters with whom I could share the load. My discovery, on sabbatical at Regent College, was the finding of fathers. In Jim Houston and Eugene Peterson I had one man who is thirty years older and another who is twenty years older than I am. Neither of them is perfect, but they are men who help us see the way ahead. I have no idea what it would feel like to win the lottery, but in spending some time with these men, listening to them and watching them, I cannot believe that winning games of chance for millions of dollars can make anyone feel richer.

A letter to Dr James Houston

Dear Dr Houston

What a good and beneficial year this has been for me. One of the reasons for this is that I have come to Regent in my early forties, halfway through my adult life and not at its beginning. This year has come right at the heart of my life. I have been in so-called full-time Christian ministry for twenty-five years and hopefully there will be another twenty-five and beyond. A significant part of this experience has been my being with and observing you.

I have observed and I have learned from you at reasonably close quarters. I have spent several hours with you in the Friday group, spent delightful time in your home, seen you interact with my wife, and listened to your heart and mind in the Chapel. I have been shaped by you and, as you will see, it has been so beneficial for me. There is, however, one thing I need to explain and reflect on.

Why was it that I took your 'Spiritual Direction' course and never took any initiative to see you personally? I have a feeling that I may have missed one of the great opportunities in my life. I think I can usually see the good things that God brings into my path, I am not known for missing opportunities. Firstly, I felt that you were already spiritually directing me even though you may not have been fully aware of it. I believe that teaching at its best is in reality mentoring on a large scale. I have had the same experience with Eugene Peterson and some other professors as I have had with you. The times of teaching have not primarily been the experience of information exchange but the interaction of hearts. In being with me in various settings you have been directing me.

Secondly, I have perceived you to be under huge pressure. Everyone wants your time, the list on your door is full, people phone you from around the world for help, and stories of double booking filter around the Atrium. The effect of this on me was to withdraw. I felt that others needed your time more than I did, people who did not have the opportunity to see you in the settings that were mine. In one of your lectures early in the course you admitted to feeling occasionally that if you had any integrity you would resign and concentrate on the relationships you had already. That story affected my decision to hold myself back, as I often feel the same in the context of Operation Mobilisation. You were sending out two messages to me: Come, I want to talk to you and don't come, I am overwhelmed. Rightly or wrongly, I chose the latter.

I have been asking myself other questions of a deeper nature. Did I hold myself back for some other reason that my heart will not admit? Was I somehow feeling vulnerable and knew your penetration would be so sharp that I chose to avoid the intimacy? I do not think so, but these questions remain on the table.

From what I have written so far, you may think that I am disappointed; in reality the exact opposite is the case, and that will become clear in the rest of this letter. What have I learned, observed and digested from you?

On the theological level, I have been profoundly influenced by the emphasis on the relational nature of the Triune God. This has all been very exciting, but I feel like a baby in seeking to grasp the implications. I am a young boy who has had a treasure for a long time, always understanding its value but who has just discovered that the true worth is way beyond his first estimate. The impact of this one emphasis will be lifelong both on me and those who look to me for any sort of spiritual leadership.

Who would have thought that an Oxford professor could be so focused on people? The popular image of intellectuals being distant from the real stuff of life may well be justified in many, but it is not so with you. With all of what you know it would be natural that you would be assertive with solutions, but I have observed you hold back more than you have shared. Your focus has been on responding to the individual in front of you rather than on explaining some grand scheme for spiritual and psychological health. What is happening at these times? I think you are praying for people as they speak and the result of that is community between God, the person and you.

You are a 'world class' listener and as such remarkably perceptive. You listen to language which is beyond nouns and verbs. The intent of your heart is not to solve problems but to perceive correctly and understand. I have noticed how people have told you some incident in their lives anticipating a direct response from you to their particular situation so that a solution would be found. It has been delightful and occasionally hilarious to see the look of horror on their faces when you have centred around another issue entirely. What they believed they were revealing with their words was not what was being revealed at all. The effect of this has been destabilisation of the person to whom you have responded. If Friday mornings were a boxing match, you would have faked a punch to the ribs, allowed a response to the ruse and floored them with a swift upper-cut; a number have been seeing stars after our sessions on Friday. How good this has been: the exposure of what we are afraid to see has been in an atmosphere of acceptance and love, united as brothers. Life does not come much better than this.

I have seen you take huge risks in the way in which you talk to people. You do not have a reputation for claiming any charismatic gifting, yet you operate with a gift which many wish they had. When you are speaking to people about their lives you often seem to trust your intuition and launch out in what looks like either wild speculation or re-markable perception. On many occasions your speculation has been seen to be God's word to that individual. It is the way you hold the gift that has been so influential on me. You do not promote your gift, you just use it. There is no roll of drums, flashing lights or magazine articles, just gift release. There have been occasions when your speculations have seemed to be inappropriate to individuals at that par-ticular moment, yet this has not seemed to trouble you. You shrug your shoulders and move on to the adventure ahead. It has been wonderful to see.

You have demonstrated the power to let go even of things that are so close to your heart. Regent is not all of what you wanted it to be, but you have not picked up your books and walked away. You are not totally invested in what you have created; you appear to be centred somewhere else. This loose grip on things is winsome and attractive. These things still matter, but they are not defining things. There are not many Christian leaders who can begin what you have begun and be satisfied with influence rather than the exercise of executive power. Few Oxford professors will leave and head out on a white-water adventure of faith, or would even think in those terms. I am sure there is a lot more to this that I do not see, but what I do see is real.

You have not been intimidated by the chaotic; rather you have embraced it. You have the ability to surf the circumstances of conversation and life, watching for the next wave which you should ride. The result of this is that you remain fresh and youthful. Often when I look at you I do not see the doctor, lecturer and founder of an institution that has influence worldwide. What I see is a young Scottish boy with all sorts of things in his pocket, collections of recent discoveries, and the glow of those possessions remaining on his face. Possibly all this comes naturally to you, but I do know that if you are going to embrace people you inevitably embrace the chaotic, a lesson that many Christian leaders have yet to learn.

One of the most exciting things about being with you is wondering where your mind is going to next. It is possible that Rita, after many years of being married to you, may not find this so exciting as the rest of us. You seem constantly to pan out from any point so that the whole environment can be understood. From you I have learned not only the importance of context but also the importance of the context of the context. Rarely have you told anyone to do anything, you have rather led them across the terrain of their lives, explaining to them the nature of what they are facing, and offering help. I have often been stunned by your conclusions and by how you have related issue to issue in a way that would never have occurred to me.

I have saved my most meaningful observation, at least most meaningful to me, to the last. You have taken on the role of father. You remind me so much of the elders at Bethshan Brethren Chapel in Southport. The elders there prayed for me as a young boy, teaching me in a way they would never have guessed. I see in you what I saw in them: not literal fathers but men of strength who could show me how to cope with realities I faced. I am particularly vulnerable to this because of the turmoil of my own upbringing and the death of my father when I was seven. You have shown an added dimension: care and compassion for my wife. How does this make me feel? It makes me feel very protective of *you*. I somehow want to make sure that *you* do not get hurt. I feel fundamentally strong and I want to make my strength available to you even though I cannot see that you need it. I suppose it is not difficult to guess where these emotions have their roots.

Thank you for Regent College and for all that you are in the lives of so many.

16

Reflections on a Friend and Brother: *George Verwer*

My first encounter with George was when I was 14. He was preaching at a convention in my hometown of Southport, England. He was in his mid-twenties and was already a ball of fire. Operation Mobilisation (O.M.) was on the British scene and he was the major architect of all that was happening through the mission throughout Europe.

What struck me about him was his youth, loudness and honesty. He was the first person I had heard seriously address the issue of sex, which was becoming an increasingly important topic for me. I liked him from a distance. He was all American and all spirit-aggression. He was clearly weak, as demonstrated by his sex stories, but had great strength. God seemed to be using a weak person and this was a new concept for me; all I had heard so far was the need to be great and very special for God to do something through you.

Ten years later I met him for the first time after I had joined O.M. and was on my way to India. I stopped him in the hallway of the Belgium Bible Institute and introduced myself. He was wearing an old coat and shoes in which his feet shuffled due to them being two or three sizes too big for him. He did not really want to talk but did ask me whether my wife was happy about us going to India. When I told him

I was not married it was not an issue, he seemed to relax a little. We met again in several locations throughout the world for a series of brief and intense conversations, which always ended with prayer.

God really wove George and me together when I was in Des Moines, Iowa. He invited me to travel with him in his bus to Cedar Rapids. During that time he zapped me with one of his specials. 'Come to England and work with me at the International Office in London,' was the offer. The job sounded a little vague, but the possibilities seemed endless. I have a low boredom threshold and life with George looked like boredom would never be an issue. He told me in a wonderfully vague way that I would become 'like a vice-president', and that sounded really exciting. I was observing at first hand what I now know to be the master of recruitment at work. His efforts would not have worked alone. I had my own agenda, and living in London, a city which I greatly love, was part of the package. It also seemed that I could preach and teach to my heart's content. Sheila and I talked about it and we were on our way. I have never seen so many people change direction after spending a short time with any one individual as I have seen with George's acquaintances. It had happened to me and I have never had a reason over the last twelve years to regret that decision. What has been deposited in me in working, praying and talking with this man?

He has taught me to live with complexity. He is a complex character, a brilliant public communicator but on occasions socially awkward. His impatience is famed and often surfaces in the small scale of social interaction. The times when I have seen him in most tension are in meetings when the leader will say: 'Why not turn around and tell the person next to you how much you appreciate them.' How is it that such a popular public communicator should struggle with small talk. His need for self-expression often forces

George to take control of public events and he tends to run a lot of what he is involved in, or else avoids involvement altogether.

He is constantly matching the needs of the world to the resources of the organization, however, in his mind, this means mobilising two-hundred-thousand cross-cultural workers over the next decade. In his head he wants no growth, in his heart he wants the whole world. He believes that I have perfectionist tendencies which cloud my judgement and he is probably right. I would have gone for a smaller Operation Mobilisation with a greater emphasis on a quality experience. He would say that it is possible to have the combination of smallness and poor quality and he is right about that. He is able to live with contradictory feelings, avoiding paralysis and maintaining his motivation.

His reputation is as a tough guy and hard driver, but that is far from the reality: he has great sensitivity. You can affect his mood by the position you take on your initial meeting with him. He has a great passion that people should have equilibrium, or, in his words, 'balance'. If you bound into his presence with exuberance, he will tell you all the problems you need to face; if you enter depressed, he will tell you how central you are to God's plans, the organization and to him. In this behaviour he reflects the tenderness and judgement of an Old Testament prophet. It is this sort of strength woven into vulnerability what makes him so endearing and an easy model to follow.

He has a strongly competitive element to his character. Depending on where the opposition is coming from he is able to shift his well-stocked verbal arsenal. He occasionally enters into win-lose scenarios. 'Them' can be the world without Christ, the non-grace-awakened church, his fellow area leaders, or the rest of O.M. if his team is under threat. I have little doubt that when he's feeling alone with his life, 'them' can be some of his very close friends. He embraces combat and I have often felt thankful that he is on my side, for he would make an awesome enemy.

He has taught me about Christian brotherly love. I do believe that if I were to fail in ministry and run for a thousand miles, his intention would be to chase me and see what he could do to help. In this he reflects the heart of God to me. He has pursued, loved and helped people who had tried every other avenue. Homosexuals, the mentally ill, failed O.M. leaders, divorced couples and newcomers to the organization have all been the recipients of his hot-pursuit tactics, which always include waves of phone calls, prayer and letters.

He has taught me to avoid the trivial. Of all the people in the world there is no one who has so clearly and so often ripped through the fantasy and triviality of my life. He is often able to do this by an inspired phrase, very rarely through systematic study and explanation of the Scripture. In the context of education he once said, 'You do not need to learn more but apply what you already know.' He is full of proverbial wisdom. These things look trivial on this typed page but in the context of friendship are very powerful.

He has taught me about generosity. He lives the paradox of having a 'simple lifestyle', which has been a historic emphasis of the organization, and he is generous at the same time. This is one of the characteristics central to my appreciation of him. He wants to be a giver. I do not know anyone who has given so much away based on so few financial resources. He has been wonderful for the occasionally mean-spirited and smug English church. If you press him, he will admit to giving his shirt and trousers away at the end of a meeting in India. Why? I think it was because someone asked and there is something in the Bible about that.

He has helped me in developing a sense of proportion. He does have a real sense of his own inability even though others do not. Often, instead of agonising over a problem, he will just move on, feeling that he has made his contribution. He will later come back if he has something more to offer. His world is one of continuous dialogue, loose ends and many problems that do not have immediate answers. It is this sense of proportion that points to the inner quality of humility. In the end his world is shaped by the knowledge that unless God does something, things are not going to get better anyway. All this is rooted directly into his prayer life.

He has been my primary mentor in organizational leadership. He has been brilliant in handling the structure of the organization. Part of his genius has been his pragmatic adaptability. The history of many organizations is painfully littered with leaders who cannot adapt: pioneers who did not know how to lead people after the initial footholds of organizational life had been established, generals who could not get out of the way and in the end were shot by their own troops. George has been able to transfer the areas of his weakness to others who are strong. There are not many who are able to trust, develop and mentor people who are a potential threat to their position in the organization, while maintaining healthy relationships in the middle of constant change. I am sure that one of the keys to his social and spiritual health has been prayer and repentance throughout the process.

He is an outstanding motivator. People observe him and want to be like him or at least have his values. The gift all seems to come from a full commitment to anything he does; his 'wimp factor' – his own phrase – is minimal, although he denies it. He is continually repentant and has no hesitation in expressing his sorrow if he has hurt you. He has also discipled people, continually giving individuals attention that they would not get from lesser people. A huge part of his motivational gift is in the fact that people believe that he is a 'man of God,' and they are right. It was remarkable to be with him in London at the meeting of many mission and church leaders which he had called. The idea was to develop a response from the missions community to the famines of Central Africa. Many key people came just because it was George who had called the meeting. Leaders who have not talked in any meaningful way in the last decade came together because of him and the challenge he placed in front of them.

I have seen his mood swings have a powerful effect on strong people. He spoke to our international leaders' gathering and began in a dark mood. The atmosphere in the room followed and what had been an encouraging time became serious and reflective. Halfway through the message he plunges through a 180-degree change of mood and is almost giggling by the end of what has become a victorious time for him. The clouds have gone, and it is springtime in his heart. At the same time, the people who were in happy equilibrium before he started his message are by now in a deep and dark frame of mind, staggered by how he is now laughing and almost dancing as he walks out. The whirlwind has come and has gone. I have learned never to trust his dark moods: they will change for the better and they often change very quickly.

Some have called him a 'prophet,' others have called him a 'modern-day Hudson Taylor'. One close friend became so addicted to his preaching that he followed him around England listening to all his messages at first hand. But what about his dark side? Does he have one? He does and he knows it better than most others.

I asked a leading preacher and author in the U.K., 'Who would you like to be if you could not be yourself?' To my astonishment he said he wanted to be George Verwer. I was shocked at this thought. I was stunned and I wanted to tell him that he did not know what he was requesting because I had seen some of the pressures of being George at close quarters. I am glad I am not George Verwer. I do not want to feel as deeply as he does. I do not want the responsibility he has. I do not want his vulnerability.

George is brave, flexible, spiritual, and continually trying to learn. He is a lion of a man with the ability to weep over a mentally ill friend and show thoughtfulness to a child. His reactions are sharp, his instincts are godly. One of the great privileges of my life has been to know him and work together as a team on the stage of the world. He is one of God's giants. George is a friend of mine; I miss him when he is not around. Perhaps the most staggering thing is that I suspect there are hundreds of people living all over the world who feel exactly like I do.

I sometimes wonder what my responsibilities to him will be in the future. He is just showing the signs of an aging process, even though his energy is far beyond most people at their best. It is likely that age will have a debilitating effect on him, as so much of his life is motion and power. One doctor gave me a theory relating to waves in the brain which seemed to suggest that George had so many of them that he would not live beyond sixty. I do not believe it even if he were right! I look forward to seeing him in old age and being a friend to him in weakness as well as in strength.

17

Global Leader:
George Whitefield

George Whitefield (1714–1770) was and remains an influential figure in the development of church life throughout the western world. It is difficult to estimate precisely his influence on us today, but he was pivotal in shaping the American church in the mid-eighteenth century.[1] Travelling seven times to America, engaging in a diversity of spiritual, social and promotional work, he considerably influenced the twentieth-century transatlantic church. With the rise of America as a world power the contribution of Whitefield seems all the more significant. When you read his life you get the feel of a man who was before his time. Whitefield was able to blend his spirituality, startling preaching, promotional skills, social interaction, use of available media and international travel in a way that looks remarkably modern.

I am drawn to him partly because of the power of the English pub. I spent a lot of my childhood being influenced by the pubs in my home town and my mother's attendance at many of them. I spent quite a lot of my time waiting outside various bars anticipating my mother's exit. I used to get packets of crisps handed out to me by some of the clients and the occasional pat on the head when people came out. Sometimes their consumption of alcohol was such that they missed my head and stumbled on the floor slurring their curses as they hit the hard surface below. George Whitefield must have known that world.

If Whitefield had been born in this century, he would have been a transatlantic evangelist of Billy Graham proportions, straddling national cultures and being influential in the transformation of those cultures. Whitefield experienced significant and radical changes throughout the course of his life: he moved from obscurity to international prominence, from life as a barman in a Bristol pub to popular international preacher. What then were his leadership gifts that enabled him to be so influential at so pivotal a time?

He had a grip on the nature of his time

Whitefield seemed to have a grip on his context and was able to integrate his gifting and spirituality in a way that influenced many people. He became his mother's assistant in an inn for a year and a half, drawing pints, mopping floors, and cleaning rooms.[2] This experience would have developed a deep sense of England's reality. It is possible that in the rough conversation of the bar he learnt about the common lot in life, which so informed his preaching. This would have been in marked contrast to his experience at Oxford, where he was to assist other students higher up the social scale than himself. He was clearly able to relate equally to these socially enhanced individuals and to those without educational advantage. Throughout his life he covered a wide social span.

Yet this ability to understand his times and culture did not remain with him for ever. Stout feels that he was not able to see things changing around him after ten years of itinerant ministry. By 1750 most of the interest in 'the great awakening' was waning, but for him nothing had changed as long as his meetings were as well attended as they were before.

It is remarkable how many movements and organizations go through the classical pattern of 'storming, norming and forming'. Whitefield appeared to have done the same. Being contemporary and at the cutting edge in one period does not guarantee relevance in the next. This is especially so for us as we crash from modernity to post-modernity and beyond. If George Whitefield was unable to cope with the pace of change, how will we be any different?

Embraced cutting-edge communication

Whitefield reinvented preaching.[3] He was able to take preaching out of the hands of the academics and locate it in theatre. While his religious contemporaries were working on theology he was developing his dramatic skills through the study of acting and reading plays. He was preparing himself for the task of transforming the narratives of the Bible into the narratives of people's lives. His primary goal in communication was not the delivery of religious information, but through the combination of the Word, drama and the work of the Holy Spirit, the personal transformation of those hearing him. He used all his considerable theatrical skills to this end.

Fortunately he was able to take all his theatrical gifting and learning into the pulpit. This co-option of what was perceived to be godless into the service of the Kingdom was vital and controversial. He demonstrated that God is able to use things considered unholy and put his glory into them, transformation taking place in the process. He was a star preacher in London at the age of twenty-four; he must have been good, really good, at preaching.

Whitefield is showing us the way here. His life is boldly saying to us that communication has to be contemporary and to fail to work in the cultural context will ensure irrelevance.

Worked various media to advantage

Whitefield was able to use both theatrical and promotional techniques. He was able to project himself without giving much thought to his reputation. Stout says that his two favourite subjects in conversation were 'the new birth and himself'.[4] He wrote and published journals. *The Weekly History* was a magazine that he published both in America for a short time, and in Scotland. His sermons were sold and he had literature projects to promote his meetings throughout his ministry.[5] He used the imagery and methods of the world of commerce for what he had to offer.[6] The matching of the preaching and promotional gifts proved to be highly successful in the building of the Kingdom of God.

Possessed substantial spirituality

There is no doubting Whitefield's commitment to Christ and the evangelization of the world, but what was the nature of his walk with God?

He seemed to have had the pulpit as a place to regain both spiritual and emotional equilibrium. He regularly preached 40–50 hours a week. Stout states that, 'as always, private failures, frustrations, and illness were best cured in the pulpit'.[7] Whitefield would not be the first or the last of preachers to need to exercise their gift for themselves as well as their audiences. Is this inappropriate spirituality in such a man? I think not. In a world where so many of our conflicts and initiatives in worship are resolved or unresolved in the middle of our own personal situations, we should have little problem in allowing Whitefield the room to do the same. He was also remarkably disciplined and ascetic making considerable personal sacrifices in an effort to enhance his spiritual life.

Developed relational skills

Whitefield possessed considerable relational skills which aided his ministry on several levels. He had significant gifts when interacting with other Christian leaders, building a powerful network of associates. His first response to intimidation was to charm and flatter; his second was complete withdrawal.[8] This is the sort of behaviour you learn if you have to deal with drunks and alcoholics, as he would have had to in Bristol.

He was much more successful than John Wesley in adapting himself to the colonial situation and won the Americans over very quickly. When disputes arose he was able to apologise, explain and move on with many preaching opportunities being left open to him. He deftly dealt with those who wanted to claim him for themselves, remaining open to all so that he might preach in many different settings. He was able to understand what was essential in his mission and shape his relationships around it.

Maintained vision and focus

George Whitefield's extraordinary vision has been described as a 'revival-driven transatlantic parachurch committed to the individual experience of the new birth'.[9] His vision was huge. This vision, arising from a generous heart, enabled his basic approach to most things to be positive.[10]

His novel vision was of a religious culture in which separate denominations were subordinate to larger unities, which was unusual for its day. Both he and Wesley played their part in the creation of a church culture open to parachurch groups formed out of denominations, although they achieved this by totally different routes. Although anti-institutional in many of the positions he took, Whitefield remained a committed Anglican while working constantly on a broad-based appeal.

His evangelistic vision was distinctly individualistic. He had a huge impact on the development of the culture of individualism through his new-birth message. Which focused on you and your personal experience of God. This emphasis has many echoes in modern-day western evangelicalism and its secular spin-off is all too obvious. It was clear vision that enabled the development of a clear focus, a distinct feature be shared with the Methodists. This vision and focus were borne out in his daily decision-making and personal discipline, shaping all his relationships. His mission absorbed him.[11]

George Whitefield was part of a spectacular move of God that was broader than his own ministry. This is a brilliant preacher who goes off for adventure and the fulfilment of a spiritual vision to Georgia when he is so popular in London that he has to take a coach from appointment to appointment to keep him from the crowd. He was an incredibly hard worker throughout the whole of his life. He faced continual misunderstanding and opposition, some of his own making, which led to persecution and almost cost him his life. He was a complex character and a considerable amount of his life is still shrouded in mystery. He chose not to found a denomination, yet his influence over British and American evangelicals is huge. I have even met an Indian evangelist who is named after him! He was a man of God of Apostolic proportions. He can show us the way to handle our futures, not perfectly but adequately.

18

Leadership in Constant Transition:
Kathi Tarantal

I first saw Kathi at a huge youth congress in Belgium in 1990. The first things that struck me about her were her confidence, her eloquence and the sharp, intelligent look on her face. She also had quite a reputation as she was pioneering work in Hungary and doing it by herself. We met again at a course which I was leading in the south of England. This was a small course of twelve people who were selected by their leaders because of their potential and promise. It was on this course that she met her future husband and now they have two healthy and energetic children. Kathi and her husband Peter – who is a talented and prominent leader himself – now lead Operation Mobilisation in South Africa. Kathi is from Nebraska, USA, and is in her late thirties.

There are particular circumstances which affect women who are gifted leaders. There are continuous theological debates in Christian circles about biblical text, culture and feminism; there is the issue of family and children; and there are men, who are usually the ones who make most of the decisions regarding women. The feelings surrounding all of this run very deep indeed. As the debate rolls on at the cognitive level it seems to me that we are often touching more primal roots.

I always had difficulty with one particular leader who worked with me on several projects. He was very gifted as a public and personal communicator, he had the best sort of Christian background available in his country of origin, and he went to one of the world's best universities. We should have got on well, but we did not. There was a continual underlying hostility, which we never did resolve. The sparks between us surfaced at a public business meeting and were noticed by a mutual friend. The friend talked to me and asked me what I was going to do about this situation; he also talked to my adversary. I decided I had to talk with the source of my conflict. We had a good chat and just decided that we were so different that this sort of thing was inevitable between us. We decided that sparking each other could be good for the flow of creative development within the group. In reality the whole thing was unsatisfactory. I could not really understand what was happening behind his eyes so we left it at that. Eight years later I discovered the real reason why he just did not like me. He felt that I was promoting women into leadership, but he never was able to talk to me about it. Primal indeed.

The way in which Kathi has dealt with a male-dominated culture has been with great skill and substantial inner resources. I have watched her in operation and it has been wonderful. She is very gifted and yet her gifting has not seemed to threaten the collection of men with whom she has had to interact. It seems to me that one of the reasons why she has done so well is that she likes men, in fact she likes people. She has respect and love for the men with whom she has worked. There is an uncluttered openness about Kathi, she is absent of hidden agendas and it seems to show in how she relates to those around her. This ability to get along with men has not been at the cost of relationships with women: she has more meaningful female friends than male. She has considerable social skills, but these were not picked up on a course or through any sort of intentional training. They come from deeper roots.

Kathi's ability with people is remarkable, particularly in the context of her past. The reality of those years she continues to face in a healthy way. She has had hard experiences that have not made her hard-hearted, but which have sensitised her to what is going on around her. In reality she is a survivor and she has all the attendant characteristics of survivors. I see in her what I see in myself as our backgrounds have similarity. We both have a desire to win, a sensitivity to criticism, and the need to be a little outstanding: all the compensations of early turmoil.

Kathi has a passion for doing things well; she is an intelligent high-achiever. The rumour is that when she moved to Hungary she learned the complex language in five months, and she has done something similar with Afrikaans. She knows how to look at a problem, wrestle with it and bring it into some sort of order that makes sense to her and to others. When she is set with a problem she is able to work it through thoroughly in the middle of advising friends, a gift not given to all.

Kathi comes from an outstanding church in rural Nebraska. It is not long in conversation before she starts to mention the names of significant people who have been her mentors and friends. The church seeks to develop people on an individual basis rather than just through Sunday attendance and affiliation. This community has had a powerful effect on Kathi, and it shows. She is constantly looking for similar relationships with the people with whom she shares her life. For Kathi, small talk is fine, but it is better if it leads to big talk. This leads her to a fresh but almost naïve questioning. I still remember her question to me, 'When did you last cry?' This struck me as a great but unusual question: not the sort of question you ask if you are uninterested in the person to whom the question is addressed. It is a lot safer to wander around the superficial and keep it there.

What has emerged with Kathi is the desire and the ability to mentor. I spoke with one very gifted woman who sees Kathi as her mentor in several areas of her life. Having had huge commitment from others she is now investing similar commitment in those who look to her for leadership. The development of these relationships does not come cheaply. A lot of mentoring goes on which is rarely seen by those who focus only on organizational life. This is the world of many women in leadership.

Kathi is a pioneer, a risk taker who steps out boldly with little structured security around her. She created the path for others to follow in planting a missionary organization in Hungary and she did most of it by herself. She took the blows of cultural adjustment, loneliness and fear in the establishing of a vibrant and meaningful mission.

I was speaking at a conference in Hungary in the summer of 1997; the conference was very exciting with three hundred young people from many different parts of Europe gathered for a week of training. I spoke several times and on each occasion there was a man in his late sixties who smiled through the whole thing. He unnerved me a little. I kept on wondering what this older man was doing at the young people's event, smiling most of the time. It was intimidating. On the last night of the conference I made reference to him being with us and he sent back an even bigger smile. At the end of the conference he told me why he was smiling.

The conference took place in a Hungarian university and the older man gave me its history. It had been built thirty years ago as a temple to Stalin, but the building site doubled as a prison. He had ridden past the site each day on his bike and saw the two thousand prisoners of conscience working on the building. Many of them lost their lives in the process of building the university. He was smiling throughout the meetings because of them. That which had been built as a temple to Stalin was now, at least for the summer, a place of Christian mission and light; the whole irony and blessing of the situation moved him deeply. Kathi Tarantal's vision and boldness had a place in opening up that wonderful moment for me and had played a part in serving the people of God in Hungary. I have recently discovered that Kathi has had considerable interaction with the family of my smiling friend.

One of the forces on women who are gifted leaders, which men know little of, is continual flux in power and position. Being married, leaving Hungary for South Africa, and having children have all had their effect on Kathi. The bold pioneer now has to focus her life on the family and this has been very difficult at times. The one who had a lot of control over her life now lives with realities which control her and she often struggles with this. She has had to be very flexible with her location and position: a flexibility which few men I know would ever seek. It has not been easy. As the children are growing Kathi is finding new areas of initiative for her considerable skills and gifts, but now, for the most part, she has to live through a sort of stillness. This is the reality for many women leaders and perhaps this is why many are not so clearly marked with the egocentric behaviour sometimes seen in their male counterparts.

Great friendship binds for life and when I stand before God and hear whatever he has to say about me, I want Kathi and her husband Peter to be in my group so we can get commendation and judgement together. I will settle for that with pleasure.

Part IV

Leaders for the Future

Introduction

Leaders have to anticipate and respond appropriately to the internal and external environment if their communities are to flourish regardless of the shape of the future. A large part of that process is understanding their own reactions and responses, the community in which they live and their relationship with God.

Although identifying individual competencies is important, it is not the primary task; leaders will have to be holistic and supple in identifying the way they form organizations in years to come. Hence the need for an adequate approach to how leaders lead their organizations. A lot of Christian leaders' strategies have failed because of intense wishing and patterns of denial. The leaders who have their concepts and spirituality rooted in Disneyland rather than revealed Scripture are going to cause considerable damage to the Christian community.

Henry Mintzberg has said the strategy 'is to craft thought and action, control and learning, stability and change'.[1] What is the 'craft' and what are the competencies required for leaders to be effective in the organizations and communities of the future?

19

Submit to the God-given Context

The Lord says to my Lord:
"Sit at my right hand
until I make your enemies
a footstool for your feet."

The Lord will extend your mighty
sceptre from Zion;
you will rule in the midst of your enemies,
Your troops will be willing
On the day of your battle.
Arrayed in holy majesty,
From the womb of the dawn
You will receive the dew of your youth.

The Lord has sworn
And will not change his mind:
"You are a priest for ever,
in the order of Melchizedek."

The Lord is at your right hand;
He will crush kings on the day of his wrath.
He will judge nations, heaping up the dead
And crushing the rulers of the earth.
He will drink from a brook beside the way;
Therefore he will lift up his head.

Psalm 110

There are certain realities that cannot be changed, regardless of our talent, networking abilities, power of speech or faith. These are the things which only God can change, and alteration will occur only when he is ready. To attempt to throw yourself in the face of certain realities is foolishness, and often an indication that you are not listening well. We cannot change gravity, day following night, the aging process, our history, or our basic humanity. The remarkable thing is that many leaders feel that they can change things which are beyond their control. With this fantasy in place they lead people towards an initially exciting world of control and power. In the process these same leaders become gods of the naïve, giving the people they lead a simplicity which in the end is deceptive and damaging. Believing the world is a certain way will not help you when you meet the truth that it is not.

I have a friend who is being led this way, led by a leader who thought he could change what he could not change. My friend was so convinced that Christians who lived a life of faith would not get sick that he would not let the concept of sickness enter his vocabulary. The whole world had to be interpreted as positive and that was defined as the life of faith. He was so convinced of the truth of this that even when he had chronic back pain he would live in denial of it, despite the weeks off from work and the continual pain. What is happening with my friend and his leader? The leader is continuing to insist that somehow this pain and sickness is not real. This is very weird stuff and not the reality as presented to us in Psalm 110.

This Psalm leads us into the God-given context which leaders have to embrace. It is a messianic psalm pointing away from David, the author, to Christ the King to come. This is a big psalm presenting us with big thoughts; it presents to us the huge context in which leaders are called to lead. Four realities are present in the psalm.

Reality One: God is in complete control

In verse one we have the image of God who is ruling over everything. We have the image of relaxed domination. God is going to demonstrate that all of his enemies will not only be at his feet but he will rest his feet on them!

Reality Two: enemies are present

Verse two explains that God's rule will take place in the midst of his enemies and not in their absence. God will extend his might while our enemies surround us. There will be problems, battles and pains which we will just have to live with until the future described in Reality One is realized.

Reality Three: continual prayer

Verse four introduces us to Melchizedek, who was the priest eternal. The picture is picked up later in the New Testament and used in reference to Christ. It is a picture of continual prayer. We live in a world of continual prayer and the centre of this prayer is not our prayer but the prayer of Jesus. The New Testament teaches us that 'Jesus prays'. Our prayer is in response to his prayer. In Eugene Peterson's words we are 'answering God' in prayer.[1] In other words, we are not the centre of the action in the cosmos. God is the centre and a key reality is the conversation between God the Father, God the Son and God the Holy Spirit.

Reality Four: God shatters his enemies

In extremely powerful and violent imagery, verses 5–7 explain the reality of the future. God will crush his enemies in his wrath; he will judge and heap up the dead and in the process crush the rulers of the whole earth. In contrast to this we get another image of a much gentler kind. God will also 'drink from a brook beside the way' and in the process lift up his head. In this picture of the end we have a reality of power and refreshment. God wins the battles and is seen drinking.

In the middle of this picture are the people of God who are described as volunteer 'troops' who arrive from 'the womb of the dawn', spread like 'dew' and are arrayed in 'majesty'. This is a picture of an unusual group of people; they offer themselves, emerge from the light, go through the process of birth into the world, look like an army, spread everywhere and nourish the land they touch. This glorious and complex picture is of the people of God. The images are as complex and rich as the people of God.

What is fascinating is the location of these people in the context of the psalm: they are located in the middle. All the huge realities of God's authority, the presence of enemies, continual prayer and enemy-shattering swirl around this group of people. They are themselves complex and wonderful, but they live in a particular context which has to be understood if we are going to understand them.

Where do leaders fit in Psalm 110? Leaders are in a confusing place. In one sense, they are right at the heart of the people of God, living out the vivid imagery. In another sense, they are in a grey world, the world between the realities surrounding them and the people of God. The reason why leadership is often so complex is that good leaders inevitably face many directions at once. There is a continual conversation between the people of God and the huge context in which they seek to live out their lives. Great leadership encounters the conversation and complexity and does not seek to simplify that which defies simplicity.

What is the context into which this psalm draws us and to which we have to submit? David leads us to the inevitable messiness of life; it will be full of paradox and confusion.

There are some forces over which we have no control and we need to realize that; leaders live between huge cosmic forces and the people they lead. To live in denial of this massive context is to lead with stupidity. If leaders deny the context given to them by God they will begin to develop the characteristics of the cult. The people who are the glorious, complex, powerful, 'womb of the dawn', need leaders who can live with the implications of submission to God – they deserve no less.

20

Understand Contradiction and Model Clear Vision

When I was a child, I talked like a child, I reasoned like a child.
When I became a man, I put childish ways behind me.
Now we see but a poor reflection as in a mirror; then we shall
see face to face.
Now I know in part; then I shall know fully, even as I am fully
known.

1 Corinthians 13:11–12

Then God said, "Take your son, your only son, Isaac, whom
you love, and go to the region of Moriah. Sacrifice him there as
a burnt offering on one of the mountains I will tell you about."

Genesis 22:2

I can see clearly now the rain has gone, I can see all obstacles in
my way. Gone are the dark clouds that had me blind, it's
gonna be a bright, it's gonna be a bright sunshiny day.

Nash, *Don't Smoke in Bed*

Complexity and ambiguity are an integral part of community life, especially for those working in an international environment. Organizations that want to be alone are not
going to be able to cope with the future as it unfolds. The
general swirl of life makes it impossible for organizations to

control every aspect. Other organizations and communities are going to smack into ours, usually at the point when it is the last thing we want to happen. Organizational life is more like bumper cars at the fairground than the hundred-metre race at the Olympics. The result of this is that so many things happen over which leaders have little control; often the initiatives of others overtake their own. Sleepless nights and stress eat away at the leaders who will not live with the reality that at some points they need to stand resolute and at others they need to flow like water.

For some evangelical leaders loss of control is difficult to face. I well remember spending some time with a church in India. They were a wonderful group of sixty people and they all seemed to be getting on well together. After a while it became clear to me that they did not meet with other Christians and it later emerged that they believed that they were a special group of Christians. They felt that when Jesus returned to the earth he would come for them first and all the millions of other Christians later! They were thus able to avoid the complexity of the real world, selecting a style and theology which would match their fantasies of isolation and ensure simplicity in the short term.

Every organization has a system within a complex network of other systems working within it. These systems – spiritual, relational, environmental, technical, psychological, financial, structural, managerial and personal – are all giving complex feedback to each other, causing considerable difficulty and blurring of focus. An awareness of the interplay and balance between these systems is central in attempts to understand what is happening. In this sense, considerable attention has to be given to everything taking place around us in the communities which we are called to lead.[1]

Attempts to seek some sort of secure equilibrium where we feel that all has to be nicely balanced are going to fail. In one sense, the really great leaders drive away from stability and into chaos. This is what happened with Moses, David, Paul and several others in the Old and New Testaments. If the organization is going to adapt and grow it has to become unstable at least to some extent. The chaos and contradiction that I talked about earlier will not be dealt with by just standing still and believing we have security. Ralph Stacey says, 'Developing new perspectives means shattering old paradigms and changing old structures – creativity requires destruction. The need for an organization simultaneously to "display fit and split" creates tension.'[2] There will only be security in a shark-like momentum towards a preferred future. In this context any sense of arrival will be dangerous. In other words, our great danger is complacency. The feelings of arrival, no matter how warm and peaceful, are fantasies which will produce destruction in their turn. The myth of the final solution will undo us.

A further complexity is a leader's need to identify strategies of interdependence with those organizations which are not her own. Accountability is no longer going to be merely focused on our own organizations, but will have to operate in relation to other organizations and communities. Networking outside your own organization will be essential for survival. There will be blurring of the edges between organizational territories, which will demand a new flexibility from leaders, and this in turn will demand new skills and vision. For Christian leaders, you would think, this should not be a problem because of an understanding of the unified yet diverse nature of the body of Christ, but often other issues dominate and cause considerable confusion.

Developing an organization which is willing regularly to ask fundamental questions about itself will create further complexity. We know how to repent from our individual faults but do our organizations and communities have the power to do the same? Christian leaders need to be more open to the impact of the Christian community on how they are doing their job. The organizational and geographical distance between the leader and many of the people they lead demands a new informality. The emphasis will not be on rules and regulations, but on creative, fresh relationships that resemble an organism rather than on organization. With this model in mind, structure will flow with reality of relationship and not dominate the community through the establishment of rigid hierarchies.

A vision which can be contextualised and communicated will be essential if people are going to cope with continual change. Leaders will need to develop an overarching sense of direction that will help to reorientate people through continual change. Seeing clearly in the middle of complexity and contradiction is one of the characteristics of good leaders. The great danger in this is that in an attempt to be authoritative we oversimplify what is complex and eventually confuse the people we are intending to help. Lord have mercy.

21

Maintain Momentum in Times of Change

We have to know when and where to stop. In a work in which
God is intensely active, we have to be cautious, reticent lest we
interfere in what we do not understand. Wendel Berry says that
he knew a barber who refused to give a discount to a bald
client, explaining that his artistry consisted not in cutting off
but in knowing when to stop.

Eugene Peterson, *Under the Unpredictable Plant*

Secular models of leadership have little to offer regarding
any concept of personal faithfulness. The pressure to make
money and stay in business has caused a reduction in any
concept of loyalty for many organizations. Even though we
are in a world of continuous and rapid change, all of what
we do is intended to be in the context of faithful service to
God and community. Faithfulness is not just living with the
inevitable; it is living in a God-context where we are able to
see what he is doing and join him in the middle of it. This is
not always easy as you can't always find where that middle
is. Often you have to lead from the dark not knowing what
God is up to in your context, even though you can see the
big picture from Scripture.

Once we have some idea of what is going on this usually
means that we have to move forward and show people how

they can do the same. Moving forward does not necessarily mean moving fast, being spectacular, or starting a new programme. Often, the way forward for Christian leaders is standing still and listening to God. Effective progress is not always related to rapid pace. A leader's reactive response to the future usually causes problems, if the reaction does not emerge from a context of faithfulness.

The skilful leader is able to work and see growth in a world of flux and stability. Within the Christian community, two dangers which hinder God-initiated growth lurk below the surface: building on the glory of an irrelevant past and star-gazing into a fantasy future that will never be. To be able to avoid both of these pitfalls we will need to be sensitive and responsive to what is happening around us.

Leaders will need to identify environmental 'fracture lines'[1] or lines of weakness and potential instability within their own community. Organizations often fail because they are not good at picking up weak signals from the insiders. These can be memos from a new person who is struggling to fit in, organizational jokes, or nicknames given to the boss. Patterns forming in the distance need to be observed. The assessment of what is happening around us needs to be a constant process. This is not so difficult to do if you live submissively and openly, but leaders have a tendency to avoid these things, especially when under pressure.

Organizations will need to be built with Ashby's law of 'Requisite Variety' in focus; this states, 'the complexity and speed of the firm's response must match the complexity and speed of the change in the environment'.[2] There must be scope within the organization to enable it to respond to every disturbance from outside. Negative and positive ripples are continually lapping around and through each organization. Adaptation requires rapid response to these trends and the creation of an organizational culture that facilitates regular flux. Change is normal and no change will need to be regarded as abnormal.

Viewing the community from the outside and not from the inside will be an important, yet difficult skill. High prices are paid for consultants who will do this job for us, but leaders need to develop this area. The process of retreat and reflection must not be neglected if our communities are to have quality leadership. Timing, creativity and discipline are crucial skills needed for this task, but even more important is the crafting and blending which enables the change to work effectively.

Ralph Stacey has helped us understand that organizations which are controlled on one side and tend towards the chaotic on the other are often healthier than they look.[3] He helps us understand that innovation does not necessarily come from equilibrium and stability; it often emerges from the edge of chaos. This is why the selection of the people you work with seems to be even more important for the future than it is today, if this particularly radical balance and contradiction is to be maintained. The assessment of someone's competence will need to measure not just skills but flexibility and growth potential. Can the people on our leadership teams and in our communities embrace and be comfortable with paradox?

This world of flux and stability is not a peaceful world as we humanly understand it; it is a world of considerable turmoil. It can be a lot of fun and agony and probably it will be both. One theology which will hold us back from this world is that which believes God's voice is only known by a sense or feeling of peace. The peace of the Lord does not always come with warm feelings in your heart. If leading people in the future is to do with a feeling of peace, then many of us are going to struggle in adapting to what is ahead.

22

Rooted in a Community of Friends: 2 Timothy 1:13–18

Cry if you want to, I won't tell you not to
I won't try to cheer you up, I'll just be here if you want me.
It's no use in keeping a stiff upper lip
You can weep you can sleep you can loosen your grip
You can frown you can drown and go down with the ship
You can cry if you want to.

Don't ever apologize venting your pain
It's something to me you don't need to explain
I don't need to know why I don't think it's insane
You can cry if you want to.
The windows are closed the neighbours aren't home
If it's better with me than to do it alone
I'll draw all the curtains and unplug the phone
You can cry if you want to.

You can stare at the ceiling and tear at you hair
Swallow your feelings and stagger and swear
You can show things and throw things and I wouldn't care
You can cry if you want to.
I won't make fun of you, I won't tell anyone
I won't analyze what you do or you should have done
I won't advise you to go and have fun
You can cry if you want to.

Well, it's empty and ugly and terribly sad
I can't feel what you feel but I know it feels bad
I know that it's real and it makes you so mad you could cry
Cry if you want to I won't tell you not to
I won't try to cheer you up
I'll just be here if you want me to be near you.
Scott, 'Cry if you want to' from *Don't Smoke in Bed*

Paul is in the final phase of his life as he writes his second letter to Timothy. He is looking down the contours of all that has happened and reacting to them in the knowledge of the closeness of death; he wrote the letter from prison in Rome. This was his second time in prison and the experience was not like the first. This was not comfortable house arrest; it took his friend Onesiphorus a long time to find him wandering around Rome and tackling complex officialdom. Paul is in chains (1:16): he explains that he is 'chained like a criminal' (2:9). He is lonely and bored (4:9–13). He has had a preliminary trial and is now ready for death (4:6–8).

The startling fact about 2 Timothy is that the whole text is a response to people. What seems to matter to Paul at the end of his life is his friends, the ones he has had and the ones he has lost. He lists them like some premier division football squad for us to notice as major players. Timothy, Lois, Eunice, Phygelus, Hermogenes, Onesiphorus, Hymenaeus, Philetus, Demas, Crescens, Titus, Mark, Tychicus, Carpus, Alexander, Priscilla, Aquila, Erastus, Trophimus, Eubulus, Pudens, Linus, Claudia, and all the brothers. A list of twenty-three people, along with 'all the brothers'.

Paul expresses his own one-liners regarding some of the people he introduces us to. We meet Alexander (4:14), the metal worker who did Paul a great deal of harm. 'The Lord will repay him for what he has done', says Paul or, more threateningly: 'God will give him what he has got coming to him', as Eugene Peterson expresses the phrase.[1] Demas is introduced to us (4:10); he loved the world and has left for Thessalonica says Paul. Mark (4:11) is rehabilitated through the phrase 'bring him with you Timothy', because he has been a lot of help. Who knows what other comments were in Paul's brain when he wrote, but which never made it into script? The whole book is written to Timothy, who had a very close relationship with Paul. Paul is in the middle of many relationships and he knows what is going on in his own heart towards the people in his life.

There are huge forces released into the community today which are driving us into ourselves and away from each other. They are nailing us down into patterns of isolation in a totally new way. We are now able to do so much on our own. With the growth of technology we are able to entertain ourselves looking at screens of different sizes and types. We can watch them in groups or in private. We are able to work the World Wide Web on our own, listen to the Walkman without help, and do our banking through the telephone, connecting with disembodied voices from who knows where. There is some distance between the world of Paul, with his reflections on people he had encountered and the virtual relationships many of us are having today. Is there any way of dealing with these forces?

Paul is at the end of his life and what matters is his relationship with his Lord (1:10), clarity regarding truth (1:7), and the people around whom his life is wrapped. Paul leads us through three distinct movements in the nature of friendship, movements which are crucial for leaders to recognize and be submitted to.

Leaders need soul friends (2 Timothy 1:13–14)

A soul friend is someone who is your friend and who is interested in all the dimensions of your life, including your walk with God. It would be easy to use other words to describe the relationship between Paul and Timothy. I could have used the word mentor or disciple, but neither conveys what I want to say. Paul and Timothy were friends, there was a lot of affection and feeling in their relationship: Paul talks of prayers, tears, longing and joy (2 Tim 1:34) in relation to Timothy.

Paul wants Timothy to be courageous and not ashamed. He wants him to put his life into significant areas, avoiding myths and not arguing over words. He wants Timothy to be ready for difficulty and suffering. He wants Timothy to preach the word and be faithful to it. These are the desires and impulses of soul friends, people who love to see you grow in all of the best dimensions of your life. These people are precious people.

What did Timothy get from Paul through this relationship? He got a pattern of how to live. Paul says to Timothy, 'What you heard from me, keep as a pattern of sound teaching' (1:13). What does he mean by pattern? Paul probably means that he wants his life to be an example or prototype for Timothy to follow. Through his own life Paul is giving an outline sketch of how Timothy is to live.

But how do you keep the sound words and the model offered by Paul? You keep or guard them through faith and love. You do not keep them by just knowing them, teaching them, or even by understanding them. An exercise of the mind will not enable you to live well; authentic spirituality works on another level, a much more intimate level.

Paul's exhortation to Timothy to 'keep as a pattern' is different from 'keeping' the law of the land. I can keep the law of the country I live in without faith and love; all I have to do is obey and I will be fine. This is not so if you are going to keep what God has given to you. It is possible to go to church regularly and be a biblical scholar and yet remain a spiritual illiterate. This is possible because you understand the message of the text but only with a cognitive grasp. This approach to a life of faith was not possible in Paul's world. Grasping, keeping, guarding what God had given to Timothy was rooted in the way he lived his life, not just in the things he understood.

Paul gave Timothy exhortation regarding what he wanted him to be and the tasks to be accomplished. Paul writes, '…set an example for the believers in speech, in life, in love, in faith and in purity. Until I come devote yourself to the public reading of the Scripture, to preaching and to teaching.'[2] The goals Paul sets for Timothy seem very high and unrealistic.

Yet, the exhortation was delivered in a context, and that context was not the world of exhortation but the relationship which Paul and Timothy enjoyed. Paul explains: 'You, however, know all about my teaching, my way of life, my purpose, faith, patience, love, endurance, persecutions, sufferings – what kinds of things happened to me in Antioch, Iconium and Lystra, the persecutions I endured.'[3] Paul was not telling Timothy to change on the basis of theological grasp alone; his appeal was primarily relational. He was explaining to Timothy that relationships, cognitive grasp and theology all blend in together if the kingdom of God is going to be built.

Timothy is exhorted to 'guard' it with the 'help of the Holy Spirit' (2:14). He has to guard the 'deposit'. He was going to guard the deposit by investing in the lives of others. This word 'deposit' always had the idea of giving someone money or valuables and getting them to keep it until your return.[4] Paul was saying keep this because it is going to matter, someone is coming back for it.

Leaders will have to deal with disappointment

'You know that everyone in the province of Asia has deserted me,'[5] says Paul. Unfortunately for Paul and the rest of us, friends do this sort of thing. Paul's Asia was the western end of Asia Minor – what we call Turkey – and this had been a place of considerable success. In reference to Paul's arguing for the kingdom of God in Ephesus, Luke writes: 'This went on for two years so that all the Jews and Greeks who lived in the province of Asia heard the word of the Lord.'[6] Things had gone well in Ephesus in the initial stages. Yet, all the wonders of the theology and practicality of the book of Ephesians resulted in ultimate desertion. This was clearly a huge disappointment to Paul.

Many of us have been abandoned in one way or another. We have been betrayed by our children, husbands, wives, organizations, countries, churches etc. There is no end to the potential of betrayal. Paul puts his focus on two individuals who betrayed him, Phygelus and Hermogenes. We do not know who they are but the speculation is that they did not come to speak for Paul in Rome when he needed them.[7]

Paul is saying that when he needed them most they were not around. Phygelus and Hermogenes had deserted, whatever the nature of that desertion. There are some people whom you relate to but, in what you can perceive as the end, it all falls apart. I can think of one individual in my life whom I would not know whether to hit or hug if he came to my door. I think he would respond to me in the same way if I went to his door. Both of us are living with feelings of betrayal and the relationship has never been resolved, and it has been many years. With both of us being English these feelings would probably be suppressed, if we ever did meet, and we would offer each other a cup of tea and a biscuit!

Resolved and unresolved conflict is part of the reality of leading. What is clear with Paul is that he still goes on doing what he knows he must do. There is no euphoric reconciliation with some of the Ephesian Christians, rather pain to be endured. The example that Paul has is his Lord: Jesus still works even in the presence of Judas. Disappointment and betrayal are part of the leadership reality, and good leaders embrace this with all of the attending pain.

Through friendship leaders will be constantly renewed (2 Tim 1:16–18)

What becomes clear in this passage is that the source of Paul's pain is also the source of his strength. Both the joy and that agony come from the same root. Paul is renewed by his friends. Timothy and Onesiphorus are very important to him. Their relationships with Paul seem to be sustaining him in the middle of the process of death.

When speaking about Onesiphorus, Paul explains that this relationship had renewed him. He describes the relationship as refreshing, shame-free and helpful. Yet, in the context of his imprisonment there is an outstanding characteristic of this renewing friendship: Onesiphorus pursues Paul. 'He searched hard for me . . .' says Paul. He is saying that he has propelled himself in my direction, he has chased after me. Other so-called friends had not done this; they had deserted.

Leaders are made for community; therefore we will be renewed by our friends. Leaders need people who will pursue them and be with them in times of shame, pressure, old age and change. What is the nature of your friendships? Do you have soul friends? Are you helping people in their walk with God and being helped?

23

Empower and Destabilize

As kingfishers catch fire, dragonflies draw flame;
As tumbled over rim in roundy wells
Stones ring; like each tucked string tells, each hung bell's
Bow swung finds tongue to fling out broad its name;
Each mortal thing does one thing and the same;
Deals out that being indoors each one dwells;
Selves – goes itself; myself it speaks and spells,
Crying What I do is me: for that I came.
Gerard Manley Hopkins, *As Kingfishers Catch Fire*

Leaders need the skill of being able to motivate and challenge people to grow and change. That demands a stable and unstable organization. The delivery of 'bounded instability', the provision of boundaries around instability is a crucial task.[1] The people we lead need to be both safe and unsafe at the same time. This is the way God leads us; he gives us a large safe space in relationship to him and then encourages us to move forward into a world of risk and faith. We need to do the same for the people entrusted to us.

People need new knowledge and the reshaping of their ideas if they are going to continue to grow. This requires regular innovation, which in turn needs a measure of instability. To do this well, leaders have to live in a large and complex world and avoid narrowness and oversimplification. We have to be aware of the climate and not just the weather. The climate is the nature of how things are, the weather is the climate delivering today's reality. The ability to focus on the economic 'climate' rather than the 'weather' has been the underpinning successful strategy of successful organizations. If the long-term is stable, you can cope with short-term problems a lot better. If I am empowered by God and community then I can face being in an unstable situation.

Leaders have to prepare people for all the conditions they face and not just the ones they would prefer. In the summer of 1995 I took several days of spiritual retreat and silence while I walked around the shoreline of Vancouver. On several of those days I walked past the marina at Spanish Banks and saw instructors teaching new windsurfers. The first day I saw them it looked easy with a gentle breeze filling the sail. The second day was totally different, with a strong wind flipping the sail and the windsurfer over at will. The third day was different again: there was no wind at all and all the windsurfers could do was lie on their boards and hope for a blow of air. The teachers had to teach them how to live in all three of these environments, and Christian leaders have to do the same.

Leaders have to release the potential of those they are called on to lead. There is no more important task than opening up doors and showing people possibilities. In one sense leaders are like the doorman at the best hotel in town: they greet warmly, open a door and display to the people going through the wonders of what is inside. It is no wonder that the Psalmist said that, 'I would rather be a doorkeeper in the house of my God than dwell in the tents of the wicked.'[2] Being a doorkeeper is wonderful work, especially when you are showing to people the wonder of God and of themselves.

The importance of the people in an organization is increasing along with the pace of change. The growth of technology is not diminishing the importance of people in healthy organizations. People who opt to be 'cogs in wheels' will not be effective or efficient models if what we are to do we do well. Everyone will have to make a contribution that is wider than just doing the job. Involvement with people, understanding their needs, individual aspirations, weaknesses, vulnerabilities and motivations cannot be left to personnel departments alone. Leaders will also have to do that themselves and not hand over the responsibility to any other agency either human or electronic. Now every leader has to be able to face the challenges of dealing with people. This will require a blend of the specialist and generalist approach to team leadership, which we talked about earlier. The lack of women in key places within the Christian community could prove to be expensive as they often demonstrate these 'people skills' to a greater extent than men. Aggression which is badly focused and cultures of domination will not result in organizations able to respond with speed, and well.

How do you help people to relish change when security and safety appear to be the dominant issues in their lives? Space has to be provided for promoting creativity, learning and innovation. That will mean allowing room for people to fail. Individuals will need time to reflect and be refreshed, allowing a more poetic model of leadership. Management models that merely control will be inappropriate if creativity is going to be stimulated. The need to develop ownership of the task is critical. That means people will have to be surrounded by inspirational lives, people who do more than just deliver a service while they are at work. Leaders will have to exemplify the living of a full life in all of its rich complexity.

Growing large in scope, while remaining close in relationships, will demand new leaders who will be able to live beyond their own personal objectives. Wrestling with huge ideas that are even bigger than the scope of the immediate task will become central to the leader's life. It is not acceptable just to use people and discard them when their task has been completed. There will be challenges ahead. Enthusiasm and strong opinion often drive innovation. A type of chaos is often the result, therefore conflict resolution becomes an important core skill for all those who want to destabilize and empower those they lead.

24

Integrate Technology into your Experience

Then Saul dressed David in his own tunic. He put a coat of armour on him and a bronze helmet on his head. David fastened on his sword over the tunic and tried walking around, because he was not used to them. "I cannot go in these," he said to Saul, "because I am not used to them." So he took them off. Then he took his staff in his hand, chose five smooth stones from the stream, put them in the pouch of his shepherd's bag and, with his sling in his hand, approached the Philistine.

1 Samuel 17:38–40

We are in the middle of rapid changes in technology. The move towards electronic mail, the possibility of remote conferencing through television and the impact of the super-highway raise significant questions. We have the possibility of highly skilled technical people who are also lonely and depressed. Focusing on the technology they use can compound their isolation. The need will be for leaders to think through how we can develop soul friendships and integrate the power of technology into our communities. The shattering caused by 'virtual' relationships will create significant pastoral challenges in the next millenium.

Developing the skills of what has been called 'helicoptering' will become important, especially if the organization does not have a clear hierarchy.[1] This is where leaders are able to move rapidly into a situation and exit at the appropriate time. This should not mean the development of shallow relationships, as long as helicoptering is related to technical solutions and not a strategy for team building. It will also be important, if not essential, to have flexible workstations and hours, especially in the international environment. The ability to identify quality information will be central to a leader's task. It is now possible to overload people with information causing demotivation. Training people in the identification of useful and non-useful information will become a core skill of leaders. A friend of mine will only read half of his email; he decides from the name of the sender and the title of the paper whether it is worth his time.

Rapid decision-making is being forced on all those who want to remain on the cutting edge of technology; this could mean a reduction in the reflection available to produce a quality decision. We are somehow going to have to produce 'community' for those inside our organizations, however that concept will be defined. It will be important that technology does not seduce us into allowing it control of strategy and relationships. My guess is that the basic need of most leaders is for someone who is a loyal friend in a world of shifting alliances and intensive tasks. The way that leaders can help their people through the stresses of the technological revolution is to be their friend in the middle of continual adjustment.

25

Embracing the Life of Prayer

Prayer, the Church's banquet, Angels' age,
God's breath in man returning to his birth,
The soul in paraphrase, heart in pilgrimage,
The Christian plummet, sounding heaven and earth;
Engine against the Almighty, sinner's tower,
Reversed thunder, Christ-side-piercing spear,
The six-days' world transposing in an hour,
A kind of tune, which all things hear and fear;
Softness, and peace, and joy, and love, and bliss,
Exalted manna, gladness of the best,
Heaven in ordinary, man well drest,
The milky way, the bird of Paradise,
Church-bells beyond the stars heard, the soul's blood,
The land of spices, something understood.

George Herbert, *Prayer*

And pray in the Spirit on all occasions with all kinds of prayers
and requests. With this in mind, be alert and always keep on
praying for all the saints.

Ephesians 6:18

Spirituality has been described as 'the combination of praying and living'[1] and as that which 'concerns the way in which

prayer influences conduct, our behaviour and manner of life, and our attitudes to people'.[2] Edward Yarnold has described spirituality in the following words. 'The imitation of Christ, which has been the theme of spiritual writers from the time of the New Testament, is not just the copying of Jesus as a model, nor the acceptance of Christ's values; it means that we share Christ's own life organically, as the scriptural images of vine and body imply, so that we grow from within into the likeness of Christ, unless by sin we distort our development.'[3] All three of these writers seem to be pointing towards the Christian life as a blend of being and doing, the way we live organically integrated with the way we pray.

For Christian leaders to lead well they need to pray well. So, what is prayer? At its most simple and deepest point, prayer is 'conversation with God'.[4] When the disciples asked Jesus how they were going to pray, he led them into conversation with God. This conversation is huge and profound, but at its essence it is talking and listening between God and his creation. Ann and Barry Ulanov lead us into the possible depths by explaining that prayer is:

> primary speech of the true self to the true God. It reaches far below words into the affects and images and instincts living in us subconsciously, into the depth psychologists call primary process thinking. Prayer makes use of all we know verbally and emotionally, our conscious secondary, process thinking, forming words and wishes sent in urgent pleas or in quiet meditations to our Lord. We speak in prayer from our most hidden heart to the hiddenness of God, in whose astonishing image we were fashioned and find our true faces. In prayer we speak to and of ourselves, of what lies heavy on our minds, of what rumbles in fear at the pit of our stomachs, of the grudges and resentments we hold behind our eyes below the surface of our outward being.[5]

Prayer has become a much more complex issue for many, but I am not sure that the complexity has helped. It seems that the more sophisticated people become in their prayer the more distant they become from God, the centre of prayer. Because prayer is at its essence relational it has to reflect the qualities of relationships. In conversations between friends there is rawness, misunderstanding, humour, love, affection, challenge, appreciation and anger. In real friendships there is the reality of life. The conversations are not manicured, stylized or manipulated, they flow with mood, atmosphere, and changes taking place outside the immediate conversation, the interruption of the phone, a crying child or a barking dog. Prayer is lived in this context if it is lived well.

If this is true, what is the place of the prayer meeting, the evangelical 'quiet time', going to church, having communion, or any prayer ritual? I think the answer is that all of these external and corporate expressions of prayer are themselves part of our ongoing conversation with God. They are vital, but they are the visual and communal expressions of what is going on already in the mystery of our life before God.

The ritual is important in maintaining a life of prayer. There have been times when I have felt that all I had as a prayer life was the external ritual of opening up my Bible and reading it, or going to the prayer meeting just because it was time to go. Sometimes God can be very quiet and many times I can be remarkably stupid in listening to his voice. It is at those moments that my external life of prayer often plays a very important role.

The weakness of many leaders, at least in evangelicalism, is that they insist on living their prayer lives on the basis of individuality. The cultural domination of self in the West is shaping our patterns of prayer more than we care to notice. There is often little sense of community in the way leaders pray. The pressure to be the super-heroic figure in leading the community of God, blocks the way to grasping the valuable resource of the community at prayer. Many leaders' prayer lives are confused, incomplete and sporadic. It is these very realities which should propel leaders into the heart of communal prayer. We are intended to join our faltering conversation with God with others, so that we will be together in one voice with the Lord who loves us all.

It is in the joining of our own conversation with God in the middle of the Christian community that we will discover the power to intercede. If you listen to God and to the community of his people you will have little choice but to take on the reality and burdens of the world. Talking and listening to God softens your heart; it makes you vulnerable, creating cracks in your make-up which you do not understand. It is the developing of these vulnerabilities that produces what used to be called 'brokenness', the sense of being in a mess before God and anticipating that he is going to put things together in the way which is best. This, in true Christian paradox, is not a place of the leader's weakness but a place of enormous strength.

26

Understand Self and Political Realities

"I am very willing to give up my leadership of my organization.
The only things I need to keep control of are money and people."
                    A Christian leader who was being asked to resign.

There is a difference between what people say and what
people do, even in – who would have believed it – Christian
organizations. Leaders are not always normal, healthy,
spiritual and objective people. It is possible that what appears to be the development of strategy could be a defence
mechanism or the operation of covert politics. It is possible
that the desire to preach or teach is really a search for
control and power.

The tragedy of space shuttle 'Challenger' has become an
illustration to my generation of leadership irrationality. After the disaster, a study was made of what was going on in
NASA at the time. The study said that 'senior managers and
engineers created at NASA a delusional system that introduced thoughtlessness on a grand scale in order to deny the
uncertainties they faced'.[1] It appears that battles relating to
power, significance and budget had a large part to play in
the disaster. NASA did not know itself as a community, and
it is not on its own.

A friend of mine was recently interviewing four people
for a job as a significant leader of a well-known Christian

organization. All of them were colleagues and one of them was going to be the boss. Each of the candidates was asked, 'How will you react if one of the other three gets the job you want?' All of them said that this would not be a problem and they would be only too happy to go with the selection panel's decision. The choice was made, and the following day the four were at war. They were unable to live with the decision and were clearly in a world of delusion and self-deception.

Leaders will have to come to some understanding of their own mixed motivations and maintain a grip on reality regarding themselves. For many the challenge is this: will we be able to be vulnerable and yet accepted as a leader within the community? To put the question another way, will it always be necessary to fake control when there is none? There is nothing so worrying as being with a driver who cannot accept that his driving is bad, because of the loss of face in the admission. Spontaneous development of groups that will be coalitions around certain specific issues will trigger feelings of threat and fear in many leaders, and it will get more intense. Living with that reality and avoiding paranoia will be a crucial factor in building a healthy organization. This is why basic spirituality is so important. To assume that pastors, missionaries and executives are all doing well, because of assumptions regarding the office they hold, is naïve in the extreme. Christian leaders have to lead while often remaining a deep mystery to themselves.

If Christian leaders themselves are not able to live within the potential chaos of being open and vulnerable, it will be impossible for that model to be effectively mentored to others and community fantasies will continue to cause confusion. We should have some sort of required reflective opportunities within the organizations of which we are members, so that we can be ready for dealing with the realities ahead. If we do not know something of what is going on in our own lives and communities, what right do we have to tell the world to be like us? Occasionally I have met leaders and got the overwhelming impression that the reason why they are in leadership is to protect themselves from the overt assessment of others. The position they hold and the role they perform is a castle to defend themselves from the onslaught of their real or imagined fears.

The ability to shape and position an organization demands a mixture of reliable gut-feeling and experience. Analysis alone is inappropriate, the leaders of organizations of the future have to make sense of a situation and explain it in an understandable way to others. This political skill demands an understanding of self. Leadership is an art form, and the blend of the various competencies in an appropriate way will make a significant difference to how a community faces its future. This, to a large extent, will depend on the inner qualities of humility and integrity being at the base of the leader's character.

It should not be beyond us to have continuous future scanning, in the way that the Royal Dutch Shell Group have had for many years, a permanent forum of 'future thinkers' seeking to outline possible futures rather than predict which one will happen.[2] The crucial thing is letting go of the past and avoiding clinging only to what we know is safe. There is no perfect answer in a changing world. We have to forget perfectionism and head for mobility, prayer, action, community, the poetic life and integrity. At best we will always be dealing with paradox, in the context of the grace of God: 'The secret of balance in a time of paradox is to allow the past and the future to coexist in the present', which brings us back to chaos, flexibility and how God sees time.[3]

27

Create a Culture and Remain a Learner

In the last analysis, I have always believed it is not so much their subjects that great teachers teach as it is themselves.
Frederick Buechner, *Now and Then*

There is no more important task for a leader than to create the culture of the group they lead. Leaders are the guardians of the way things are done, how people are handled, the way the group approaches God, what the group will do, and the way forward. Culture formation is right at the centre of the leadership task. Edgar Schein's model[1] of artefacts, espoused values and basic underlying assumptions outlines the areas of research which attempt to encompass an organizational culture. For Schein, artefacts are the visible organizational structures and processes; espoused values are the strategies, goals and philosophies and the basic underlying assumptions are the unconscious, taken-for-granted beliefs, perceptions, thoughts and feelings. It is through watching these things that you will be able to perceive something of the reality around you. Attempts made at changing a culture have often failed because the leaders did not address the basic underlying assumptions of the people they were seeking to lead.

As Schein puts it: 'The bottom line for leaders is that if they do not become conscious of the cultures in which they are embedded, those cultures will manage them.'[2] Crucial to building that culture is formation of a sense of history, the corporate memory of the group.

There have been many attempts to re-write history so that a group of people can be led in a certain direction. Some Japanese have tried occasionally to ignore their treatment of Korea; the British have been coy regarding their history in India. Both countries have made choices with regard to which history they want to present to future generations. Most military organizations make little reference to what someone was or did before they joined up and this is usually because they do not want people's personal histories getting in the way of following orders. If people know their roots and who they are they will be able to face a preferred future that relates to history. Organizations come from some-where, even those of the new and fast-paced world built around the new technologies.

One of the dangers for the leader in the future is skilled incompetence, the ability to do well what should not be done at all. The perception of many people in Europe is that the European Community is dominated by skilled incompe-tence. The perception is that highly paid and well-trained people run administrative machines that are just doing the wrong things.

This phenomenon will usually emerge when we respond to tasks with inadequate paradigms of how we learn. The danger is that we avoid the basic assumptions which form the context of our decisions. The result is a loss of freshness and an inability to ask the most fundamental questions about what we are doing and why we are doing it. This is where the community must play its part. It is from the ques-tions and provocation of an unrelenting friend that I am going to face my own assumptions and learn.

We are going to have to learn how to discuss the topics we resist due to their threat to us. Often it is our 'inscape' that gets in the way of us honestly looking at reality. What happens is that politics, arrogance and ignorance provide effective blocks to healthy learning and, in its turn, to incompetence. Very often, we are not aware of this going on inside ourselves and in the lives of the people we are working with, as Ralph Stacey said: 'The real causes of poor strategic management – the learning process, the political interaction and group dynamic – remain stubbornly undiscussable.'[3]

Leaders are powerful people; they are often more powerful than they realize. How they deal with their power will have radical influences on the people around them. I have recently had a conversation with Billy and Jan. They are an extremely pleasant couple with so much to offer to any organization they might work with. After four years outside the influence of a particular Christian leader, they are still affected by his deeds, words and the culture which he created. It was difficult to hear their subsequent story through the tears of the conversation. It was a story of intimidation, of authoritarian and task-oriented leadership. Whatever else happened, it was clear that the leaders of the organization were not grasping the negative impact which was being made through them on those they led.

Being effectively mentored should help leaders to respond to their communities with flexibility. This will, at least, enable them to be knowledgeable about their inadequacy. Billy and Jan were still bitter about the experience they went through, and continue to struggle even though they have good jobs and each other. To generate a quality culture and at the same time continue to grow and learn is the calling of the Christian leader.

The expectations of stakeholders need to be considered in culture building. These are the people who may not be an immediate part of the organization or community but who will be affected by the decisions of insiders. The domination of the stakeholders' felt needs could produce a static culture; the ignoring of them could produce a loss of identity. Leaders who want to build something significant have to take account of these people; they are ignored only at the leaders' peril.

28

Be Continually Going

The range of our possible sufferings is determined by the
largeness and nobility of our aims. It is possible to evade a
multitude of sorrows by the cultivation of an insignificant life.
Indeed, if it be a man's ambition to avoid the troubles of life,
the recipe is perfectly simple. Let him shed his ambitions in
every direction, let him cut the wings of every soaring purpose,
and let him assiduously cultivate a little life, with the fewest
correspondences and relations. By this means, a whole
continent of afflictions will be escaped and will remain
unknown.

J.H. Jowett, *The Price of Enlargement*

The Lord said to Abram, "Leave your country, your people
and your father's household and go to the land I will show
you."

Genesis 12:1

"Therefore go and make disciples of all nations, baptising them
in the name of the Father and the Son and of the Holy Spirit."

Matthew 28:19

Leaders can easily live small lives. They may have vision for
their particular area of concern, but once outside the area
with which they are familiar they are lost. People who are

huge and visionary in one area can be tiny and impotent in another. It is a kind of deformity. Most of us are aware of the leader who leads their organization well, but has no vision for family, or who works so hard at making money they cannot really work out how to use it effectively. Part of the answer to this dilemma is the process of going, the act of momentum.

The church is intended to be a growing organism, it is intended to move and develop. It is Jesus who told the church to 'go' and yet many of his disciples are focused on the process of staying. Why is this so?

Christian leaders have to live within the paradigm of both coming and going. Jesus commanded the church to 'come unto me all who are weary and heavy laden', and to 'go into all the world and preach the gospel'. He put us in a context of both staying and going; they are intended to be together. Continual staying without going leads to stagnation; continual going without staying leads to exhaustion. We often stay because to go is perceived as unsafe, but is there any safety more substantial than responding to God's call to go?

I have had the experience of going at all sorts of levels. There have been the great and easily identifiable movements. Transferring from secondary school to technical college at fifteen (without my mother's knowledge), leaving home at eighteen to work in the bland factories north of London, arriving at Bible college at nineteen, church planting in Manchester at twenty-one, driving to India at twenty-four, pastoring in London at twenty-six, heading for Pakistan at thirty-one, working with George Verwer at thirty-three. There has been a lot of going. There have also been the initiatives which have been more subtle and profound. They may have had less profile, but their meaning has been more than geographical relocation.

What does this mean? It means that what drives Jesus should drive us, it means that the vision Jesus has should also be ours, it means that what moves Jesus moves us, his burdens are our burdens, his joys are our joys. What then is the drive, vision and heart of Jesus? What moved him to come to earth, be born, live a life as an outsider and die such a horrific death? The answer is people: the world and the six billion individuals in it. To be like him means that his self-giving is the way in which we are intended to go.

Leaders are intended to be mobile

This does not mean dashing everywhere at ever-increasing speed; it does mean ever looking towards new horizons ahead of us and making decisions in the light of what we see. For Abram this meant leaving his country and setting out to his much more risky future. For many this means geographic relocation to other cultures and languages. For some this will mean staying in one place and doing a long-term quality job where the horizons will be the development of individuals, who will in turn learn what it is to go. A characteristic of good leadership is that it moves and transforms through responding to the call of God.

Leaders are intended to teach and bless the nations

God told Abram that 'all the nations of the earth will be blessed through you'. Jesus told the disciples to go to the nations and 'teach them to obey'. Both of these statements are full of authority, they proclaim, they do not apologize. The idea is a simple one. The people who were intended to lead the community of God forward were to be among the peoples of the world, teaching them and blessing them.

Once this is grasped, there is no telling where this may lead. For one friend it meant starting clinics in Asia, for another providing housing for refugees, for another teaching people to read, for another teaching blind people Braille and how to walk down a street, for another the performing of facial surgery on deformed babies, for another teaching farmers how to run a business. In their own unique way they are out teaching and blessing the nations.

Leaders are intended to obey

The glory of a Christian leader is not rooted in charisma or ability; it is rooted in the capacity to obey. For Abram and the early disciples the context was obedient response to the clear command of God. It was God who set up the frame of reference for them to respond to him, and not the other way around. This submission is one of the most exciting things on earth.

When one of my friends grasped this and followed it through it meant teaching the piano to the family of a President whose country had gone through considerable turmoil. Another friend ended up on the floor of a car with a gun pointing at his head as a terrorist asked him what he was doing in this part of the Asian town he was walking through. After a few days had gone by these terrorists released him telling him that they loved him. For one group of my friends it meant that they were given two goats and a monkey for services rendered in central Sudan. To do this sort of thing well you need to have two things clear: obedience to God is basic, and you cannot take this on alone.

Leaders need to go if they are to live healthy lives

A man died in England recently and a post-mortem was held to try and work out why. It revealed nothing. Doctors then decided to examine the man's behaviour up to and including the day he died. What they discovered was that this man was addicted to television. For several months before his death he just watched television all day and all night. He only stopped to perform the basic functions of life. The doctors believe that his body could not take this sort of abuse; a machine that was intended to move was not moving and in the end decided to close down.

Fish are made for swimming, frogs are made for jumping, and leaders are made for going. If we do not catch the spirit of this, we live unnaturally, we make nothing and nothing is made. We need to go as much for our own sakes as for the needs of the world. The peoples of the world need leaders like this.

Part V

The Process of Restoration

29

The Relocation of Zechariah

Zechariah asked the angel, "How can I be sure of this?"

Luke 1:18

> Every eye must weep alone
> Till I Will be overthrown
>
> But I Will can be removed
> Not having sense enough
> To guard against I know
> But I Will can be removed
>
> Then all I's can meet and grow,
> I am become I Love,
> I have Not I Am Loved,
> Then all I's can meet and grow.
>
> Till I Will be overthrown
> Every I must weep alone.

W.H. Auden, To Chester Kallman

"His name is John."

Luke 1:63

Zechariah was a professional religious leader. Like all of his type, both before and since, he was living his public life in the context of his private anxieties. He was a priest living through the reality of childlessness. His life was a good life; he and his wife Elizabeth were blameless in their walk with God and observant in the ways of the law. Yet, Zechariah is about to go through a process of restoration and have his priorities and worldview relocated. The disturbing thing is that although he loved and served God, he was not good either at hearing what God had to say, or the way in which he said it. This condition is not unknown or uncommon among today's leaders; in fact it remains one of our greatest challenges.

Zechariah was in a most privileged position, chosen to go into the presence of the Lord as a representative of the people. It is here, at the very pinnacle of his ministry, that his world is reframed. It became clear that something was wrong with Zechariah. He needed to go through transformation to become the man that God wanted him to be. What was wrong with this God-fearing leader? What was Zechariah's problem?

In the middle of his priestly task an angel appears to him and starts to tell him the stunning plans of God. Zechariah hears that he is going to have a son, who will bring joy and delight to him and the community. His son, John, will drink no alcohol and will be filled with the Holy Spirit at birth. John is going to be the catalyst for the restoration of the nation and prepare the way of the Lord. This is wonderful, absorbing, exciting, all-embracing stuff. What is Zechariah's response? It is the muted response of a leader missing the point. You can almost hear the dull thud of his response landing on the floor. Instead of an obedient and joyful response, Zechariah comes out with, 'How can I be sure of this?' It is clear from what he says that he and God are singing from a different song sheet and it is time for Zechariah's relocation.

Behind Zechariah's question about assurance he is really saying, how can I control this? Questions of control are often questions which lack trust. When he should have been experiencing a state of wonder or even concern, as was the case with Mary in similar circumstances, what he wants is more data. Zechariah's lack of faith did not allow him to trust and see what God was going to do. Therefore God begins to work on him to get him relocated to the right place.

Leaders are expected to be in control and many go on courses and seminars, spending thousands of dollars, pounds, rupees and marks to be able to be just that. Control is a vital part of a leader's life, things have to get organized, projects have to be run, plans and visions earthed. Yet, you can sometimes discover that the desire to grasp, understand and control leaves you unable to align your will to the will of God. You can work for God and not trust him an inch, allowing him no latitude in the shocking and surprising work he sometimes needs to do. How does God relocate Zechariah and deal with his desire to know and control? How does God cause Zechariah to see the sort of things he should be seeing?

God takes control

If you have played sport, asked a woman to marry you or had to confront someone, you will know that timing is everything. Zechariah had a dreadful sense of timing, missing entirely what God had to say. When you read around this passage you see that Simeon, Anna, Mary and Elizabeth were all able to keep pace with what God was doing, but this was not the case with Zechariah. He appears to be rooted to the spot, unable to extricate himself from the mire of his own preoccupations and his need to know. God's solution for Zechariah is to immobilise him in such a definite way that he would have no doubt where the real authority lay.

Time is very important to leaders. Dashing from meeting to meeting, living under the pressure of deadlines, and trying to prioritise so that all may be accomplished is the stuff of leadership. Sometimes the only way for God to break into this is to take our control away from us. He leans into us so that we feel the power of his frame, imposing his strength as Father. He has a wide variety of ways to do this; sickness, aged parents, financial pressures, organizational agendas, a new child, or someone with whom we work who does not go at our pace – all these are available to God. These and many other things all intersect with our lives and let us know that we are not in control: God is.

God imposes dumbness on Zechariah

God closes Zechariah down in one area to open him up in another. Through dumbness God shuts off his ability to communicate, giving him unexpected and unwelcomed stillness. It seems that Zechariah was probably deaf as well. What happens to Zechariah is a sort of retreat. What happens to him also happens to us when we enter times of retreat. We discover a new perspective, a new way of seeing and listening. Retreat is closing you down so that you may be opened up. God closes Zechariah's hearing and speaking down, making him more dependent on sight, touch and smell. He is now in the hands of God in a unique way. What does he see through this deprivation?

Zechariah's world is now the world of the female. Elizabeth, Mary and two swelling bellies: that is what is looking him in the face. His world of dumbness was a world of pregnant women and the action taking place inside them. What is this female, pregnant, womb-world? It is the world of formation and intimacy. As he watched these women he would have been able to see what God was doing and how he did it. What was happening within these wombs was a picture of what God was doing in Zechariah. As Jesus and John were being formed in the womb so Zechariah was being formed in the silence imposed on him by God. Zechariah's condition could not be rushed; wombs and the plans of God have their own season.

God gives the attention to others

Before God imposed dumbness on Zechariah he was a leader of prominence. As God begins to relocate him through deprivation he discovers that all the attention and the control have been moved away from him. Zechariah is no longer at the centre of the action; he has become a sideshow in the unfolding of God's purpose. God has done this in a very humiliating way for a Middle Eastern man; he has given the attention to women.

Leaders often adore the centre; their gift and self-love draw them into the vortex. Many of us love being in the centre of the information flow, understanding all of what is going on around us while giving it our own shape and spin, feeling the buzz of significance through being at the pivot. But, to teach us intimacy and the way he works, God has to move us to the side, even if it is only for a time, so that we can learn who is really in control. The fascinating thing about this story is that Zechariah only receives release from his own womb of dumbness when he aligns himself with the words of his wife. His journey has relocated him from control and unbelief to submission to the community, the desires of God, and a life of obedience, a journey mandatory for leaders who wish to lead well.

What follows is pure joy. Elizabeth and Mary have their babies and Zechariah has his own birthing, his Benedictus. This is one of the most glorious and celebrated songs of worship, truth and exaltation in the New Testament and in church history. It is full of perspective, redemption, depth, history, optimism and future. It emerged from a leader who had learned that God was in control, released from his desire to know and able to embrace his future.

The future is coming fast and the challenge to be the leader able to face it is constant and real. We will only be able to face the future if we are located in the same place as Zechariah. In a world where many leaders are focused on their own self-enhancement, projected image and drives to control, Jesus teaches us another way. It is a way of being powerful when you are weak, tough when you're soft and huge when you are small. It is absolutely subversive of the model given to us by a self-besotted world. Our challenge is whether we can embrace our future in a way which shines out the wonder of God. We live in a world so desperately in need of leaders who, while not perfect, are men and women who grasp that in themselves they are inadequate but in relationship to Father, Son and Spirit are fully adequate to lead into the future.

Endnotes

Introduction

[1] The advertising of Nike at the 1996 Atlanta Olympic Games gave the idea that coming second was failure.
[2] P. Johnston in *Operation World*, 1995, claims that 32% of the world's population considers itself Christian.
[3] I use this word frequently. See especially chapter 2. It is a word coined by Gerard Manley Hopkins, picked up by Eugene Peterson and reworked by me to apply to persons, not just things.

Part I

Chapter One

[1] Matt. 27:11.
[2] Matt. 27:19.
[3] Matt. 27:13.
[4] John 18:36 quotes Jesus, who said, 'My kingdom is not of this world.'
[5] Mark 15:8, 'The crowd came up to Pilate and asked him to do for them what he usually did.'
[6] Matt. 27:20.
[7] Matt. 27:15.
[8] Matt. 27:19.

9 Pilate's Praetorian soldiers, the actual torturers, were auxiliaries, not Roman legionnaires, and would have been recruited from the non-Jewish surrounding areas, e.g. Phoenicia, Syria, and possibly Samaria.

10 Matt. 27:24, 'When he saw he was getting nowhere . . . he said it is your responsibility.'

11 Matt. 27:24.

12 This was useless symbolism, an attempt to wash away his own sin. Hand washing was not a Roman but a Jewish custom. It could have been an attempt to mock the crowd.

13 John 19:11, 'You would have no power over me if it were not given to you from above.'

Chapter Two

1 John 13:3.

2 Is this why many seminary experiences are so disappointing?

3 G. Morgan, 1986, p. 159.

4 John 10:30, 'I and the Father are one.'

5 John 12:10, '. . . for I did not speak of my own accord, but the Father who sent me commanded me what to say and how to say it.'

6 Eph. 1:4.

7 See Chapter Two.

8 I think that the popularity of the prosperity movement is based on these inner fears.

9 Heb. 11:16.

Chapter Three

1 Neh. 2:1.

2 Neh. 1:1–3.

3 F. Buechner, 1991, p. 66.

4 Neh. 2:4.

5 E. Peterson, 1989, p. 37.

6 Neh. 1:7–9.

[7] 1997.
[8] Neh. 2:11–17.

Chapter Four

[1] In the album *Ten Summoner's Tales*.
[2] 1 Chr. 11 and 12.
[3] 1 Chr. 11:1.
[4] 1 Chr. 11:15.
[5] 1 Chr. 11:12–14.
[6] 1 Chr. 11:17.
[7] 1 Chr. 12:2.
[8] 1 Chr. 12:8.
[9] 2 Sam. 11.

Chapter Five

[1] Luke 10:2,3.
[2] An important proviso to this is that different cultures have alternative ways of dealing with authority. It is important to look carefully at the context and background of non-western organizations before they are written off as authoritarian.
[3] Luke 10:5–12.
[4] Luke 10:12–14.
[5] Luke 10:16.
[6] Luke 10:3.
[7] Luke 10:17.
[8] Luke 10:21.
[9] Luke 10:24.

Chapter Six

[1] Dan. 1:2.
[2] Dan. 1:3–5.
[3] Dan. 4.
[4] Dan. 1:10.
[5] Dan. 2:20–23.

[6] G. Morgan, 1986, p. 202.

[7] Bobby Kennedy performed the role of 'mindguard'. When other members of the cabinet felt unease regarding the strategy he would approach them and explain that the President wanted them all to pull together.

[8] This is when all the information offered from outside the group is believed to be invalid, just because it is offered from outside the group.

[9] E. Schein, 1992, p. 15.

[10] S. Sondheim: Rilting Music Inc., Admin by W. B. Music Corp.

[11] Dan. 1:8.

[12] Dan. 4:8. Nebuchadnezzar states, 'He is called Belteshazzar, after the name of my god, and the spirit of the holy gods is in him'.

[13] 1 Sam. 17.

[14] 1 Sam. 21:13.

[15] Acts 23:6,7.

[16] Matt. 10:16.

[17] S. Covey, 1989, p. 21–23.

[18] Job 28:28, 'The fear of the Lord – that is wisdom, and to shun evil is understanding'.

Part II

Chapter Seven

[1] P. Drucker, 1994, p. 3.

[2] C. Handy, 1990, pp. 40–41.

[3] C. Handy, 1990, p. 5.

Chapter Eight

[1] P. Drucker, 1994, p. 9.

[2] C. Handy, 1990, p. 26.

[3] P. Drucker, 1994, p. 182.

[4] P. Drucker, 1994, p. 27.

[5] P. Drucker, 1994, p. 75. 'The largest may have assets of over US$80 billion and the smallest US$1 billion.'
[6] P. Drucker, 1993, p. 78
[7] P. Drucker, 1993, p. 11.
[8] P. Drucker, 1994, p. 45.
[9] C. Handy, 1990, p. 112.
[10] C. Handy, 1994, p. 24.
[11] C. Handy, 1990, p. 124.
[12] J. Naisbit, 1994. He makes constant references to the importance of the Chinese in shaping the future.

Chapter Nine

[1] C. Handy, 1990, p. 76-81.
[2] C. Handy, 1994, p. 117.
[3] P. Drucker, 1994, p. 56.
[4] P. Drucker, 1994, p. 89.
[5] C. Handy, 1990, p. 128.
[6] C. Handy, 1990, p. 132, 'Whereas the heroic manager of the past knew all, could do all and could solve every problem, the post-heroic manager asks how every problem can be solved in such a way that develops other people's capacity to handle it. It is not virtuous to do it this way, it is essential.'
[7] P. Drucker, 1994, p. 93.
[8] P. Drucker, 1994, p. 92.

Chapter Ten

[1] C. Handy, 1990, p. 32.
[2] C. Handy, 1994, p. 49.
[3] C. Handy, 1994, p. 16.
[4] C. Handy, 1994, p. 16.
[5] C. Handy, 1994, p. 18.
[6] P. Drucker, 1994, p. 57.
[7] P. Drucker, 1994, p. 57.
[8] C. Handy, 1990, p. 7.

[9] C. Handy, 1994, p. 10.
[10] C. Handy, 1994, p. 38.
[11] P. Drucker, 1994, p. 59–60.

Chapter Eleven

[1] P. Drucker, 1994, p. 107.
[2] P. Drucker, 1994, p. 109.
[3] C. Handy, 1990, p. 148.
[4] C. Handy, 1990, p. 142.

Chapter Twelve

[1] P. Drucker, 1994, p. 141–156.
[2] J. Naisbit, 1994, p. 9.
[3] J. Naisbit, 1994, p. 11.
[4] J. Naisbit, 1994, p. 23.
[5] J. Naisbit, 1994, p. 26.
[6] J. Naisbit, 1994, p. 14.

Chapter Thirteen

[1] See M. Weisbord, 1987, p. 6.
[2] D. Schon quoted by M. Weisbord in 'Toward Third-wave Managing and Consulting', in W. French, C. Bell Jr. and R. Zawacki, 1994, p. 66.
[3] J. Naisbit, 1994, p. 17.
[4] J. Naisbit, 1994, p. 21.
[5] J. Naisbit, 1994, p. 271.
[6] T. Peters, 1992, p. 32.
[7] C. Handy, 1994, p. 219.

Chapter Fourteen

[1] P. Drucker, 1994, p. 142–143
[2] J. Naisbit, 1994, p. 99.

³ P. Drucker, 1994, p. 195.
⁴ P. Drucker, 1994, p. 214.

Part III

Chapter Seventeen

¹ F. Lambert, 1994, p. 227, 'While Whitefield did not leave a new denomination or even a lasting institution, he left an indelible imprint on American society.'
² D. Jeffrey, 1994, p. 280.
³ A. Dallimore, 1990, Vol.1 pp. 103–130.
⁴ H. Stout, 1994, p. 102.
⁵ H. Stout, 1990, p. 145.
⁶ F. Lambert, 1994, p. 52. He had the help of the gifted William Saward to develop the promotional aspects of his ministry. On p. 47 Lambert states, 'Although Whitefield found much in the market place to criticise, he also discovered a framework for restating the gospel in a vocabulary familiar to his audiences. He often cast his theology in mercantile terms – shopping, insuring, banking, selling.'
⁷ H. Stout, 1994, p. 170.
⁸ H. Stout, 1994, p. 18.
⁹ H. Stout, 1994, p. 205.
¹⁰ His vision never extended to the development of an anti-slavery campaign even though he was committed to explaining the new birth to those in slavery.
¹¹ D. Jeffrey, 1994, p. 285.

Part IV

¹ H. Mintzberg, 1989, p. 38.

Chapter Nineteen

¹ E. Peterson, 1989, *passim*.

Chapter Twenty

[1] R. Stacey, 1993, chapter 6.
[2] R. Stacey, 1993, p. 104.

Chapter Twenty-one

[1] G. Morgan, 1990, p. 175.
[2] R. Stacey, 1993, p. 125.
[3] R. Stacey, 1993, chapter 7.

Chapter Twenty-two

[1] E. Peterson, 1993, p. 450.
[2] 1 Tim. 4:12–13.
[3] 2 Tim. 3:10–11.
[4] R. Earle, 1978, p. 397.
[5] 2 Tim. 1:15.
[6] Acts 19:10.
[7] W. Hendriksen, 1976, p. 283.

Chapter Twenty-three

[1] R. Stacey, 1993, p. 213.
[2] Ps. 84:10.

Chapter Twenty-four

[1] G. Morgan, 1986, p. 86–87.

Chapter Twenty-five

[1] G. Wainwright, 1986, p. 9.
[2] G. Wakefield, 1983, p. 362.
[3] E. Yarnold, 1986, chapter 2.
[4] A. and B. Ulanov, 1986, p. 31.
[5] A. and B. Ulanov, 1986, p. 31.

Chapter Twenty-six

[1] L. Hirschoron, 1988, p. 5,6.
[2] See P. Schwartz, 1991.
[3] C. Handy, 1994, p. 61.

Chapter Twenty-seven

[1] E. Schein, 1992, p. 16–18.
[2] E. Schein, 1992, p. 15.
[3] R. Stacey, 1993, p. 185.

References

Buechner, F., 1991, *Now and Then*, San Francisco: Harper.

Claxton, G., 1997, *Hare Brain Tortoise Mind*, London: Fourth Estate.

Covey, S., 1989, *Seven Habits of Highly Successful People*, Sydney: Simon and Schuster.

Dallimore, A., 1989 & 1990, *George Whitefield: The Life and Times of the Great Evangelist of the Eighteenth-Century Revival*, Vol 1&2, Edinburgh: Banner of Truth.

Drucker, P., 1994, *Post-Capitalist Society*, New York: Harper Business.

Earle, R., 1978, *The Expositor's Bible Commentary: 2 Timothy*, Grand Rapids: Regency Reference Library.

Fawcett, A., 1971, *The Cambuslang Revival*, Edinburgh: Banner of Truth.

French, W., Bell, C. Jr., and Zawacki, R., ed. 1994, *Organization Development and Transformation: Managing Effective Change*, 4th edn., Burr Ridge, Boston, Sydney: Irwin.

Handy, C., 1990, *The Age of Unreason*, London: Arrow.

Handy, C., 1994, *The Empty Raincoat: Making Sense of the Future*, London: Hutchinson.

Handy, C., 1993, *Understanding Organizations*, 4th edn., London: Penguin Books.

Hendriksen, W., 1976, *New Testament Commentary: 1&2 Timothy*, Edinburgh: Banner of Truth.

Hirschoron, L., 1988, *The Workplace Within*, Cambridge, Massachusetts: MIT Press.

Jeffrey, D., ed. 1994, *English Spirituality in the Age of Wesley*, Grand Rapids: Eerdmans.

Johnstone, P., 1996, *Operation World*, Carlisle: Paternoster.

Lambert, F., 1994, *Pedlar in Divinity*, Princeton: Princeton University Press.

Mintzberg, H., 1989, *Mintzberg on Management: Inside our Strange World of Organizations*, New York: Macmillan.

Morgan, G., 1992, *Images of Organization*, London: Sage Publications.

Morgan, G., 1990, *Riding the Waves of Change: Developing Managerial Competencies for a Turbulent World*, Jossey-Bass Management Series, ed. W. Bennis, R. Mason and I. Mitroff. Oxford: Jossey-Bass Publishers.

Murray, I., ed. 1960, *George Whitefield's Journals*, Edinburgh: Banner of Truth.

Naisbit, J., 1994, *Global Paradox*, London: Nicholas Brealey.

Peters, T., 1992, *Liberation Management*, New York: Knoph.

Peterson, E., 1989, *Answering God*, London: HarperCollins.

Peterson, E., 1993, *The Message*, Colorado Springs: Havipress.

Schein, E., 1992 *Organizational Culture and Leadership*, 2nd edn., Jossey-Bass Management Series, ed. W. Bennis, R. Mason and I. Mitroff, San Francisco: Jossey-Bass Publishers.

Schwartz, P., 1991, *The Art of the Long View: Planning for the Future in an Uncertain World*, New York: Currency Doubleday.

Senge, P., 1993, *The Fifth Discipline: The Art & Practice of The Learning Organization*, London: Doubleday, Century Business.

Stacey, R., 1993, *Strategic Management and Organisational Dynamics*, London: Pitman Publishing.

Stott, J., 1973, *The Message of 2 Timothy*, Leicester: Inter-Varsity Press.

Stout, H., 1994, *The Divine Dramatist: George Whitefield and the Rise of Modern Evangelicalism*, Grand Rapids: Eerdmans.

Tofler, A., 1980, *The Third Wave*, London: Bantam.

Ulanov, A. and B., 1986, *Prayer as Primary Speech*, in C. Jones, G. Wainwright, E. Yarnold (eds.), *The Study of Spirituality*, Oxford: Oxford University Press.

Wainwright, G., 1986, *Types of Spirituality* in C. Jones, G. Wainwright, E. Yarnold (eds.), *The Study of Spirituality*, Oxford: Oxford University Press.

Wakefield, G., ed. 1983, *The Westminster Dictionary of Christian Spirituality*, Philadelphia: The Westminster Press.

Weisbord, M.R., 1994, 'Toward third-wave managing and consulting' in W. French, C. Bell Jr., and R. Zawacki, *Organisation Development and Transformation: Managing Effective Change*, Burr Ridge, Boston, Sydney: Irwin.

Yarnold, E., 1986, 'The theology of Christian spirituality' in C. Jones, G. Wainwright, E. Yarnold (eds.), *The Study of Spirituality*, Oxford: Oxford University Press.

Metaphors of Ministry
Biblical Images for Leaders and Followers
David W. Bennett

*"Down through the centuries church leaders have studied
the Gospels to discover patterns of leadership
development that can be applied to their own context.
Yet the word 'leader' does not appear in the Gospels . . .
Could it be that leadership has more to do with learning
to follow than learning to command, supervise, or
manage? On right attitudes than on mastery of certain
skills? . . . Many of the insights we need are embedded in
the images which Jesus used to describe his followers."*

David Bennett examines all the many images and
metaphors in the Gospels relating to how disciples follow
Jesus, and in turn influence others. Then he moves in to
survey much of the evidence to be found in the images of
the rest of the New Testament. Finally, he draws some
judicious conclusions for an understanding of Christian
leadership in our own day.

**Dr David W. Bennett ministered in Californian churches
between 1969 and 1988, and is currently Senior Pastor of
Mountain Park Church in Lake Oswego, Oregon.**

ISBN 0-85364-719-4

paternoster
press